Moving Beyond Personal Loss to Societal Grieving

Moving Beyond Personal Loss to Societal Grieving

Discussing Death's Social Impact through Literature in the Secondary ELA Classroom

Edited by Michelle M. Falter
and Steven T. Bickmore

ROWMAN & LITTLEFIELD
Lanham • Boulder • New York • London

Published by Rowman & Littlefield
A wholly owned subsidiary of The Rowman & Littlefield Publishing Group, Inc.
4501 Forbes Boulevard, Suite 200, Lanham, Maryland 20706
www.rowman.com

Unit A, Whitacre Mews, 26–34 Stannary Street, London SE11 4AB

British Library Cataloguing-in-Publication Information Available

Library of Congress Cataloging-in-Publication Data
978-1-4758-4383-5 (cloth)
978-1-4758-4384-2 (paperback)
978-1-4758-4385-9 (electronic)

∞™ The paper used in this publication meets the minimum requirements of American National Standard for Information Sciences—Permanence of Paper for Printed Library Materials, ANSI/NISO Z39.48–1992.

Printed in the United States of America

Contents

Foreword

Empathy is the most mysterious transaction that the human soul can have and it's accessible to all of us, but we have to give ourselves the opportunity to identify, to plunge ourselves in a story where we see the world from the bottom up or through another's eyes or heart.

—Sue Monk Kidd, *The New York Times*

The smoke hung in the air like nothing I had ever experienced. In fact, everything about the world was unfamiliar—and terrifying. It was September 14th 2001 and I was on my way to meet with colleagues who were assigned the daunting task of training mental health professionals to help those affected by the terrorist attacks. As a psychologist, my work has always focused on children and adolescents confronted with trauma—death, illness, and disaster—from large-scale public tragedies like the bombing of Pan Am 103 and the Challenger explosion to the very personal and almost invisible devastation of parent and sibling loss. September 11th was different.

The 9/11 attacks occurred during the first week of the school year and tested teachers and students in ways unimaginable. Teachers are the first line of defense for our youth. They are critical to facilitating important conversations sparked by texts and events that speak to life's most challenging experiences. Entering classrooms and forging alliances with teachers was not new to me, yet I still struggled with two questions. For teachers and students who lived through the chaos and tragedy of 9/11, how do we help them heal? For those who were at a distance, how can they come to understand, to empathize with others?

I found the answers on the pages of classic and contemporary young adult literature. Some books offered comfort and familiarity; others allowed students and teachers to explore the horrors of a dangerous world. By the end of

September, a group of authors contributed their work to new book responding to the events of September 2001, *911: The Book of Help*. It was the first YA title published after 9/11. Pat Scales wrote the teachers' guide and I wrote the guide for parents and professionals. At that moment, I knew that YA literature would be more important than ever.

From my work with students in classrooms and therapeutic groups I've found that the best books are not only well-written but tell a story, not about a singular problem or event, but about the lives of the characters. These are not books that tell stories through a rose-colored lens with happy endings; these are stories where relationships might be fractured as well as supported. Characters emerge as friends, role models, storytellers and reliable advisors. There is opportunity for self-revelation, problem solving and social support. Understanding the links between the characters' lives and the authors' lives, and ultimately the readers' lives offers insight into the most difficult situations. When we read together as a group, it is easier to talk about difficult and painful issues. The characters, the authors and the teacher become part of the conversation; young people find their voices . . . strong and authentic.

It gives me great pleasure to tell you about *Moving Beyond Personal Loss to Societal Grieving: Discussing Death's Social Impact through Literature in the Secondary ELA Classroom*. The chapters of the book you are about to read will take you on a journey through some of the most extraordinary and provocative texts—loss and bereavement, war, disaster, violence, and racism to name just a few of the powerful topics. The authors have written with passion and clarity on how to best to use these books and engage young people in thought-provoking conversations. This volume will take its rightful place on your desk and on library bookshelves. It is an invaluable resource. Let me preview just a few of the many highlights.

There are summaries, strategies, insights, references and concrete materials for your classrooms, libraries or communities. Chapter authors emphasize advice and cautions as well. Why cautions? Because we never know what exists in the personal histories of the students in our classrooms. We must also confront our own experiences. Self-care, for you and your students, is crucial. Be aware of how your experiences, reactions and thoughts may influence how you present and react to the material in the classroom. Enlist a support system, talk about the texts, and explore the accompanying activities and your reactions to them.

From the first pages, the 21 contributors introduce us to the essence of grief and loss and what it means to young people. For adolescents, bereavement signals an end to the life they knew. Their identities and ultimately their search for intimacy are forever changed. How many young people are affected by the death of an important person in their lives? In 2009 the National Research Council and the Institute of Medicine, using U.S. Social Security Administration data, found that each year 3.5 percent of children under the age 18 experience the death of a parent. However, this number is incomplete, as it doesn't include siblings, grandparents and other significant people in a young person's life. In addition, rates can be variable and rise when there are national disasters such as the terrorist attacks of September 11, 2001, war, and now the opioid epidemic.

What is grief and how do we process it? What does it look like? What do we say to someone who is grieving? Maybe our presence is enough. It is not always about saying the perfect words or any words at all. These are important questions for students. The chapter authors offer substantive strategies for class discussions and activities based on the texts and additional readings and materials.

Because literature offers a complexity of circumstances, characters, and interactions, we become more skilled in understanding people and their intentions. We expand our capacity to be empathic. Nussbaum (1998) suggests that the type of imagination triggered by literary reading allows us to walk a mile in a stranger's shoes. Yet, it is only through meaningful discussion that we can truly appreciate what it means to take that path if it is possible at all. Hearing the stories of others, as painful as they might be, encourages us to examine ourselves—to think about our relationships with others, and our lives in general.

Conversations surrounding death and grief prompt thoughtful and sometimes uncomfortable questions. The chapter contributors offer suggestions that are not only creative and appropriate to the texts, but also sensitive to the needs of young people. There are several caveats that may serve you well as you embark on these conversations. As a foundation, be aware of the students' cognitive, emotional, and social development and how they process death and absence. Recognize that there are myths that surround death and grief in our society: the need to define stages, to measure healing after loss, to search for closure, and to erase painful images.

Phases or stages of grieving suggest there is a prescribed, optimum way to work through grief, and that one can only move forwards or backwards. This is not true. Grief is a journey that begins with loss and takes many twists and turns. The grieving process is shaped by a number of factors: our previous experiences, attachment to significant others, the nature of the loss experience, age, and the support of people in our lives. The process is much more circular, like a feedback loop.

The use of the word closure in the context of grief surfaced in media reports after Timothy McVeigh's sentencing and execution for the Oklahoma City bombing in 1995. Journalists wrote that the families' search for "closure" would come to an end with McVeigh's death. It was not true. It is human nature to find a way to end our pain. The identification of one signature event that pronounces 'no more suffering' may be wishful thinking. Grieving is one of the greatest human challenges—it is both universal and unique. The real work of integrating a loss into the tapestry of one's life is a life-long process. Grief does not go away, it changes and evolves over time.

Finally, be cautious of others who may be eager to erase our history. Society wants people to feel better—no pain or sadness. By editing sights and sounds that might remind us of the tragedy, we erroneously think people will feel better. There is a danger in hiding or removing reminders of those we have lost—no matter how long ago. It feels as if the people and places never existed, as a result we deny our own history.

There are events on the world stage that significantly change our lives. For many adults and young people in particular, these events can be confusing or frightening or both. Adults, in an effort to protect young people from the horrors of a dark and troubled world, may try to delete these life-altering experiences from our collective history. We fear upsetting the younger generation and are concerned that we won't be able to talk about this material in meaningful and age-appropriate ways. Fortunately, the literary titles captured on the pages of this groundbreaking book and the authors' thoughtful and sensitive contributions, have given us exactly what we need. I can't think of a better resource than *Moving Beyond Personal Loss to Societal Grieving: Discussing Death's Social Impact through Literature in the Secondary ELA Classroom* to accompany you on this important undertaking.

Donna A. Gaffney
Psychotherapist and Educational Consultant
Author of *Seasons of Grief, Helping Children Grow Through Loss*

REFERENCES

Cart, M. (Ed.). (2002). *911: The book of help: [Authors respond to the tragedy].* Chicago, Ill: Cricket Books.

Lee, F.R. (2014, January 14). Giving voice, and finding her own, *The New York Times*. Retrieved from https://www.nytimes.com/2014/01/07/books/sue-monk-kidd-tackles-race-in-the-invention-of-wings.html

Nussbaum, M.C. (1998). Poetic justice: The literary imagination and public life. *Political Theory, 26*(4), 557–583.

Social Security Office of Retirement and Disability Insurance. (2015) Old Age, Survivors and Disability Insurance. Number of children and total monthly benefits, by type of benefit, December 1940–2013. Social Security Administration, Washington, DC. Retrieved from https://www.ssa.gov/policy/docs/statcomps/supplement/2014/5f.html#table5.f4

Acknowledgments

I wish to first and foremost thank my family for supporting me in all my endeavors, personally and academically. I would also like to thank all of my colleagues, including all the teachers and students I have had the pleasure of working with and teaching alongside of, and especially my coeditor Steve Bickmore for his continued encouragement, mentorship, and support. Finally, I would like to acknowledge those lives who have immeasurably touched me in a multitude of ways but are no longer with us in life: my grandmother, Rosella Kuechler, who was the strongest and kindest woman I knew; my beautiful niece, Claire Marie Falter, whose short life filled our hearts with much love; and my former students, Layana Al-Abbad and Lee West, who left this world way before they should have. Their impact on my life and those around them will never be forgotten.

—Michelle M. Falter

I would like to thank my parents, John and Diane Bickmore, for the amazing support I have had all my life—for the books and the safe environment in which to read them. I can't thank Dana enough for letting me talk about "the best book ever" when I finish reading another great YA novel. I would like to thank everyone who has helped me with Dr. Bickmore's YA Wednesday. It is a labor of love that helps me think about new ways to encourage kids to keep reading. It does not exist without readers or without professional colleagues-teachers, librarians, graduate students, mentors, and academics who provide such insightful posts. Special thanks go to my coeditor, Michelle Falter. She wrote a post in response to the Netflix's version of *Thirteen Reasons Why* that turned out to be the inspiration and the driving force for this project.

—Steven T. Bickmore

Introduction

Steven T. Bickmore

Two households, both alike in dignity,
In fair Verona, where we lay our scene,
From ancient grudge break to new mutiny,
Where civil blood makes civil hands unclean.
From forth the fatal loins of these two foes
A pair of star-cross'd lovers take their life;
Whose misadventured piteous overthrows
Do with their death bury their parents' strife.
The fearful passage of their death-mark'd love,
And the continuance of their parents' rage,
Which, but their children's end, nought could remove,
Is now the two hours' traffic of our stage;
The which if you with patient ears attend,
What here shall miss, our toil shall strive to mend.
(Shakespeare, Wright, & LaBar, 1959, p. 1)

From the beginning, Shakespeare warns us that there will be violence, death, tragedy, and grief. Yet, as I taught the play over and over again to class after class of ninth-grade students, I didn't begin by discussing how these topics might affect my students. Just as it was introduced to me, I focused on the structure of art, and not on the aesthetic response that might be generated by the words (Rosenblatt, 1938/1995). I was more concerned with high art, structure, and engendering literary appreciation. I wanted them to notice that the opening lines were a sonnet. A sonnet written by a master of the genre. That fourteen lines could summarize a plot, could set the stage, and describe our tasks as literary critics and, sadly, not as humans engage with emotion.

I didn't spend as much time as I should have discussing that revenge, grudges, violence, family disruption and lack of communication, murder, and suicide were going to be the focus of our three-week journey through the pages of the play. I know now that in each class, there were students who were suffering from the list of injustices that Shakespeare highlights. In reality, many of these issues were and are difficult for me.

I am blessed to have not known much of extreme violence in my life. I do know about loss and grief. I was divorced and have watched my children struggling through the missteps of their parents. Even as I write this, my aging father suffers with a terminal lung disease from no fault of his own. His condition affects my mood, my temperament, my work, and, in realty, my interaction with others. Nevertheless, I carry on. I show up at work. I write, I teach, and I interact with students and colleagues while many are unaware of the beginnings of a new grief creeping into my life. I try to move forward, just as many of my former students did.

In this edited book, and the one that is its companion, *When Loss Gets Personal: Discussing Death through Literature in the Secondary ELA Classroom*, Michelle and I have strived to collect a group of chapters that teachers can use to walk their students through the emotional minefield that they will inevitably encounter. We are at our best as teachers when we see our students as individuals with deep emotions, with hopes and dreams, with successes and failures and not just as individuals who must pass an end of course test. We believe that literature can help us variously experience difficult situations.

In this volume, the authors of the fourteen chapters encourage teachers to confront death and grief as it appears in larger societal contexts that does the first volume. For example, school shootings, war, AIDS, racial violence and intolerance, and natural disasters are some of the large events and conditions that not only bring death to an individual but also are often of such immensity that more than an individual or a family is affected.

The chapter authors treat death as represented in the young adult (YA) novels they have selected as the real and oppressive burdens they are. Rather than explore a literary work only in terms of its craft (Bickmore, 2005), the authors deal with the strong emotions that each death or condition produces. Indeed, they are interested in the ideas and ideology (Hollindale, 1992) in addition to the craft. They offer teachers instructional tools to help students not only master standards but also confront emotions directly as an integral part of their lives and of the literature they are studying.

OVERVIEW OF THE BOOK

The book is divided into four sections: Grief and Facing Mortality, Murder, Mass Tragedies, and War and Genocide. Each section contains chapters that focus on one (in a couple cases, two) selection of YA literature that is used to address the category in a specific way. Certainly, there are many more books that could address this category. We invite teachers to read carefully and see the authors' selections as representatives of a type. The activities are varied and in most instances can translate smoothly with appropriate modification to another work of literature, a different grade level, or an alternate social economic classroom setting.

The first section, "Grief and Facing Mortality," contains three chapters that capture death and grief in distinct ways. In chapter 1, Mark Lewis focuses on the novel *Elsewhere* (Zevin, 2005) to discuss two binary oppositions: life-death and adult-adolescent. The approach assumes that youth are capable thinkers about complex topics, and that discussions about death and dying, adulthood and adolescence, are vital to building healthy relationships and understanding life and death.

In chapter 2, René Saldaña, Jr., invites readers to study death and mourning through characters in the liminal phase of their rites of passage, and how, through role-playing, readers can begin to conceptualize current or future loss in their own lives when needed. In the final chapter, James Joshua Coleman uses the graphic novel, *Pedro and Me* (Winick, 2000), to address an era of loss through the early years of AIDS diagnosis, experimental treatment, and tremendous loss.

The second section is labeled "Murder." Certainly, murder occurs across socioeconomic demographics, but all of the three chapters focus on books with race at the center. They echo the cry from the Black Lives Matter and the We Need Diverse Books movements. In chapter 4, Stephanie P. Jones uses *All American Boys* (Reynolds & Kiely, 2015) to discuss the concept of spirit-murder, a reminder that death does not mean a loss of life but rather a loss of humanity through the novel.

Tiye Naeemah Cort continues this theme in chapter 5 with a presentation of how students might contend with the emotions of death and behavioral manifestations of grief. She uses one of the most celebrated debut YA novels, *The Hate U Give* (Thomas, 2017), with its homage to Tupac's death and the legacy of his work. In chapter 6, Jackie Mercer examines Chris Crowe's *Getting Away with Murder: The True Story of the Emmett Till Case* (Crowe, 2018) to talk about death and race. How do students critically analyze nonfiction texts to identify prejudice, bias, and blatant misinformation as a result of horrific acts?

The sensibility of the third section, "Mass Tragedies," was heightened during the book production. The horrific mass shootings in Las Vegas and in Parkland, Florida, at Marjory Stoneman Douglas High School punctuated the initial drafting of the chapters and forced even more teachers to deal with mass loss. In Las Vegas, many students returned to school Monday morning uncertain of the whereabouts of some of their relatives. The effect on a community is devastating, but teachers show up and deal with students in horrific limbo. They are first responders, and communities assume that they will know how to care for students.

Lindsay Schneider considers Kathryn Erskine's novel *Mockingbird* (Erskine, 2010) in chapter 7. She discusses Caitlin's search for closure after her brother is fatally shot during a school shooting. Students who experience these mass shootings either personally or vicariously through social media or endless news cycles need teachers who can escort them through their fears, anxiety, and grief.

In chapter 8, Shelly Shaffer, Amye Ellsworth, and Kellie Crawford present activities using *This Is Where It Ends* (Nijkamp, 2016) to explore different perspectives of students at a school shooting. Each activity moves students toward a deeper understanding of traumatic events. Jennifer Dail and Shelbie Witte in chapter 9 take on a large-scale trauma—not mass shootings, but as the result of a natural disaster. Using *Drowned City: Hurricane Katrina & New Orleans* (Brown, 2015), they remind us that hurricanes and other natural disasters might strike at any time as we witnessed in 2017 with Harvey, Irma, and Maria in Houston, Florida, and Puerto Rico, respectively.

The fourth and final section of the book is labeled "War and Genocide." With five chapters, it is the largest section. Americans are not unfamiliar with the ravages of war, but we often do not stop to recognize how immersed some adults and children are in its physical manifestations and how the affects can continue when one is removed from the battlefield. In chapter 10, Gretchen Rumohr-Voskuil and Deborah Vriend Van Duinen explore the teaching of *The Things They Carried* (O'Brien, 1990) through activities that explore the author's use of experimental and various storytelling techniques.

Leilya Pitre and Steven Bickmore position a study of war on the home front in chapter 11 by focusing on one of the most widely used books in American high schools over the last fifty years, *A Separate Peace* (Knowles, 2000). At the time of publication in 2018, American families have been sending fathers and mothers and sons and daughters into battle for seventeen years. It is naive to assume that the effects of these missions are not evident in the students we teach.

In chapter 12, Janine Julianna Darragh and Ashley S. Boyd explore ideas for teaching Ishmael Beah's *A Long Way Gone: Memoirs of a Boy Soldier* (Beah, 2007) in the high school classroom, focusing on the themes of death in war and global responsibility. Crystal Chen Lee and Cathline Goulding use chapter 13 to provide resources for teachers and secondary teacher educators to engage students in the emotions associated with death in Holocaust literature. Focusing on dialogue, they use *Maus* (Spiegelman, 1986) and *Night* (Wiesel & Wiesel, 2006) as touchstone texts to talk about death in historical accounts.

To conclude, Sarah J. Donovan explores *Refugee* (Gratz, 2017) and encourages teachers to know their teen readers and trust that they can bear the sorrow, despair, and resilience of the most unimaginable stories of our lives. Teen readers need a place and space to process these experiences, and book groups position teen readers side by side to experience the discomfort and offer comfort in the heartbreak.

REFERENCES

Beah, I. (2007). *A long way gone: Memoirs of a boy soldier* (1st ed.). New York: Farrar, Straus and Giroux.

Bickmore, S. T. (2005). Language at the heart of the matter. *ALAN Review, 32*(3), 12–23.

Brown, D. (2015). *Drowned city: Hurricane Katrina & New Orleans*. Boston, MA: Houghton Mifflin Harcourt.

Crowe, C. (2018). *Getting away with murder: The true story of the Emmett Till case* (Revised and updated Speak edition. ed.). New York: Speak.

Erskine, K. (2010). *Mockingbird (Mok'ing-bûrd)*. New York: Philomel Books.

Gratz, A. (2017). *Refugee* (1st ed.). New York: Scholastic Press.

Hollindale, P. (1992). Ideology and the Children's Book. In P. Hunt (Ed.), *Literature for children: Contempory crticism* (pp. 19–40). London; New York: Routledge.

Knowles, J. (2000). *A separate peace*. Austin, TX: Holt, Rinehart and Winston.

Nijkamp, M. (2016). *This is where it ends*. Naperville, IL: Sourcebooks Fire.

O'Brien, T. (1990). *The things they carried* (1st ed.). Franklin Center, PA: Franklin Library.

Reynolds, J., & Kiely, B. (2015). *All American boys* (1st ed.). New York: Atheneum Books for Young Readers.

Rosenblatt, L. M. (1938/1995). *Literature as exploration* (5th ed.). New York: Modern Language Association of America.

Shakespeare, W., Wright, L. B., & LaMar, V. A. (1959). *The tragedy of Romeo and Juliet* (New ed.). New York: Washington Square Press.

Thomas, A. (2017). *The hate u give* (1st ed.). New York, NY: Balzer + Bray, an imprint of HarperCollinsPublishers.

Wiesel, E., & Wiesel, M. (2006). *Night* (1st ed.). New York, NY: Hill and Wang, a division of Farrar, Straus and Giroux.

Winick, J. (2000). *Pedro and me: Friendship, loss, and what I learned* (1st ed.). New York: Henry Holt.

Zevin, G. (2005). *Elsewhere* (1st ed.). New York: Farrar, Straus and Giroux.

Part I

GRIEF AND FACING MORTALITY

Chapter 1

Disruption of Adolescent-Adult and Death-Life Binaries: The Experiences of Elizabeth Hall in *Elsewhere*

Mark A. Lewis

A prevailing understanding of children and youth in Western society relies upon a view of innocence in which young people need to be protected from the "adult" realities of life, including death and dying (Stallcup, 2002; Šubrtová, 2009). This perspective, however, is a relatively new understanding of children and youth. As recently as the 1800s, death and dying were viewed as a "natural part of a child's life" because it was understood that youth experienced it regularly, and this perspective was reflected in the literature written for youth in this time period (Šubrtová, 2009, p. 1).

Yet, throughout the 1900s, a more protective view of children and youth grew out of national worries over the "wayward" lives of children and adolescence, which led to shifts in political, legal, and educational policies aimed at supporting, but also controlling and surveilling, the lives of youth (Lesko, 2012). For example, literature aimed at young people rarely addressed taboo topics— including sexuality, war, abuse, and death—in the first half of the 1900s. This trend reverted after the World War II, and, once again, literature written for children and young adults discussed all of these topics, and more (Russell, 2015).

However, many adults, including teachers, continually grapple with how best to introduce and discuss such aspects of living and dying with youth (Pytash, 2013). Therefore, this chapter, focusing on Gabrielle Zevin's *Elsewhere* (2005), aims to present instructional possibilities to build productive classroom spaces to discuss issues related to adolescence and adulthood, and life and death.

SUMMARY OF *ELSEWHERE*

Zevin's (2005) novel begins with the protagonist, Elizabeth (Liz) Hall, waking up on a ship bound for Elsewhere—a land for the dead—after dying in a car accident shortly before her sixteenth birthday. As a dead-narrator, she shares her struggles reconciling with her death at an early age, missing her family and friends, and accepting her new "living" situation in the land of the dead. Also, in Elsewhere, the dead age backward until they are once again babies and reborn into new lives. Yet, despite aging backward, they continue to gain life experiences, including finding a new professional avocation, establishing new friendships, and falling in love.

For instance, when Liz turns nine (again), she really has "lived" twenty-one years, and, in her six years in Elsewhere, she builds a romantic relationship with Owen. He died when he was twenty-six, but when he meets Liz, he has already been in Elsewhere for nine years, so he is seventeen but has "lived" thirty-five years. So, they are close in biological age—fifteen and seventeen—but have a larger gap in experiential age—fifteen and thirty-five. However, such relationships that do not follow traditional age-based norms are commonplace in Elsewhere.

Therefore, Zevin has provided a story in which both conventional notions of human growth and one-way, linear understandings of a life-death progression are destabilized (James, 2009). Teasing out these notions, as well as discovering other perspectives on growth, death, and adolescence, is the primary purpose of the proposed instructional ideas for developing a curriculum for teaching and reading *Elsewhere* in the English language arts classroom.

POSITIONING YOUTH TO CRITIQUE ADULT-ADOLESCENT AND LIFE-DEATH BINARIES

Designed for the middle school classroom, these teaching ideas begin with the assumption that youth are capable and critical thinkers about complex topics (Lewis, 2014), and do not need to be shielded from reading and telling stories related to such topics, including grief, murder, fear, and death (Bosmajian, 2002; Harju, 2009; Stallcup, 2002). Connolly (2012) further argues that many youth display remarkable resiliency and hope during traumatic events, especially in response to the loss of loved ones.

The overarching goal of this approach to teaching and reading *Elsewhere* is to develop what Strehel (as cited in Harju, 2009) identifies as "grand conversations." A grand conversation positions youth and adults as equal members of the discussion in order to provide a place where diverse cultures and social statuses can meet without judgment. In other words, a grand conversation needs to be "open, honest, equal, and reciprocal" (Harju, 2009, p. 18) between students and teachers, adolescents and adults.

Such a space can be difficult to create, particularly with discussions about sensitive topics like death and dying, so Harju (2009) suggests that adults reflect on their own views and worries about death in order to not limit how young people might develop their understandings. Further, adults in a grand conversation need to be cognizant about how they present their views so as not to silence any alternative views youth might hold. Yet, they also need to share their experiences with death to establish an open discursive space in which talking about death and dying can be discussed in safety.

Moreover, it is important to not assume that adults have more knowledge or a healthier perspective about death and dying than youth, and that relying on the opposite assumption—namely, that adults are necessarily more wise simply because they are older—can divide teachers and students into two distinct groups, ones with knowledge and ones without, which can devolve into a didactic approach to teaching (Harju, 2009). Therefore, these instructional ideas are designed for both youth and adults to enter into an equitable discursive space in which all are learners, and all are teachers.

These literary tasks are based upon the assumption that the primary instructional setting is a small group, such as a book club, with the goal for group members to discuss individual reactions and responses to the story, views about the story's themes, and personal connections between readers and the text. The approach begins with a prereading activity on binaries, followed by an ongoing during-reading response journal, and ends with a postreading mapping activity. Of course, each activity should build upon each other in order to craft complex understandings of growth and death.

Prereading: What Are Binaries?

Since binary oppositions are a central concept to this approach to teaching *Elsewhere*, it would be vital to begin with an exploration of this concept prior to beginning the novel. There are numerous videos and slideshows available on the Internet that provide effective entry points. A favorite is included in box 1.1 at the end of the chapter, which outlines the socially constructed nature of language, provides concrete, student-friendly examples (e.g., using the hero-villain and good-bad binary in comic books), outlines how different cultures place more value on one side of the binary, and relates the concept to reading literature.

After showing the video, students could begin brainstorming other binaries common in popular culture, such as television series, movies, and advertisements. For example, they could discuss how the series *Suits* relies (mostly) on a traditional male-female binary in which men have power because they are deemed stronger and more intelligent. Through such an activity, students are demonstrating their skills at using characterization and point of view to analyze larger literary themes.

Once the students have a good list, ask them to discuss which side of each binary tends to be given more value in U.S. society. In order to address diverse social and cultural backgrounds as well as expand students under-standing of diversity, it would also be important to explore societies where the value lies differently in a binary opposition than in U.S. society. For example, the Mosuo in Tibet follow a matriarchal tradition in which the head of the household is the oldest female, and lineage is traced through the female side of the family, which differs from traditional Western views of a male-female familial binary.

A final way to scaffold the understanding of binaries would be to ask students to analyze a short, short story for its use of the concept. This instruc-tional task addresses several common literacy standards, such as drawing inferences and using textual evidence to support literary interpretations and conclusions. "Dead Men's Path" by Chinua Achebe (1953) offers a high-quality example for this step (see box 1.1 for a link to the story).

Achebe's story tells the tale of a new headmaster attempting to revitalize a school in Nigeria. White missionaries assigned him to complete this task, which included a reform movement to rid the community members of their "pagan" beliefs. The headmaster also brings his wife to teach in the school, and there are clear gender roles expressed by him to his wife. The story, there-fore, has numerous examples of binary oppositions for students to identify, including male-female and academic-oral epistemological traditions.

Once the students indicate their clear understanding of binary oppositions, use the discussion on differing values about binaries and the short story analysis to extend the students' understanding on how such constructions can be harmful and debilitating. This step is key because it prepares the students to be successful in identifying the problematic binary oppositions of adult-adolescent and life-death present in *Elsewhere*.

During Reading: The Affective Response Journal

The primary instructional task for the students to complete during reading is the use of a three-column, affective response journal (adapted from Lewis, 2014). In the far-left column, the students would record a particular quota-tion from the novel. In the middle column, they would provide a brief plot summary to provide context and help them recall that information for a future discussion. In the far-right column, they would write a response explaining what they thought, wondered, or felt about the quotation (see table 1.1). The students should be asked to focus primarily on moments when they notice a binary opposition working in the story.

Teachers should model a journal entry from early in the novel in order to scaffold the process, as well as continue to complete their own journals as they read (or created before the novel study begins) in preparation for the small group discussions. In this way, teachers are honoring the process of creating grand conversations because they are establishing that everyone has the same preconversation responsibilities. Moreover, by creating and sharing their own affective response journal, teachers would demonstrate to students their desire to be an equal contributor to the group.

Each time the small group meets, the journals would provide the catalyst for creating an open conversation about what these quotations reveal about traditional and alternative perspectives on growth, life, and death. Table 1.1 provides several sample entries from the first third of *Elsewhere*. Each entry exemplifies how a focus on the relationship between adolescence and death can work to complicate binary positions.

Table 1.1. Sample Affective Response Journal Entries

Direct Quotation from Text	Plot Context	Affective Response
"'Don't you watch the news? All young people become perfect students when they kick the bucket. It's a rule.' Liz wonders if her death made the local news. Does anyone care if a fifteen-year-old girl gets hit by a car? 'The Great Jimi Hendrix said, "Everyone loves you when you're dead: once you're dead, you're made for life'" (Zevin, p. 32).	A new friend, Curtis, in Elsewhere discussing his philosophical views of life and death with Liz, particularly as an adolescent.	I wondered if what Curtis said was true about how people view the death of young people. I thought the Hendrix quotation was smart, but unfortunate since someone should be able to enjoy their success while alive.
"I'LL NEVER GO TO COLLEGE OR GET MARRIED OR GET BIG BOOBS OR LIVE ON MY OWN OR FALL IN LOVE OR GET MY DRIVER'S LICENSE" (Zevin, pp. 50–51, emphasis in original).	Liz lamenting her death at an early age.	I thought Liz's screaming was funny because of the mix of things she named. I also felt sad for her, which I guess is one reason why people get sad about the death of anyone, but especially young people.
"I think you'll find . . . that dying is just another part of living, Elizabeth. In time, you may even come to see your death as a birth" (Zevin, pp. 78–79).	Liz receiving advice from her Elsewhere acclimation counselor on adapting to life in Elsewhere.	I felt confused about this advice because I don't understand how a death could be a birth, even in Elsewhere where the rules are different.

(Continued)

Table 1.1.   (Continued)

Direct Quotation from Text	Plot Context	Affective Response
"'I'M DEAD!' she yells. 'Dead . . . is little more than a state of mind. Many people on Earth spend their whole lives dead'" (Zevin, p. 86, emphasis in original).	Liz arguing with her Elsewhere acclimation counselor, which he counters with a statement about how people often "live."	I felt Liz's frustration. I also thought that her counselor was right. I know many people who waste their lives, which could mean they are already "dead."
"'I think of [life and death] like a tree, because every tree is really like two trees. There's the tree with the branches that everyone sees, and then there's the upside-down root tree, growing the opposite way. So Earth is the branches, growing up to the sky, and Elsewhere is the roots, growing down in opposing but perfect symmetry'" (Zevin, p. 109).	An Elsewhere resident, Esther, shares her philosophical stance on the relationship between life and death with Liz.	I wondered if Esther's description of the tree could be accurate. Could life and death be reflections of one another? Or, doesn't death come after life?

For example, the Hendrix quotation and the acclimation counselor's perspectives reveal a more recursive understanding of life and death. The quotations in these entries also illustrate how the story disrupts a linear understanding of people aging from adolescence into adulthood since Elsewhere residents understand getting older as also getting younger. Through the completion of these journals, students would be illustrating their skills in establishing their connections to the characters, as well as demonstrating their comprehension of specific plot events that are important to their literary interpretations.

Postreading: Mapping Recursively

Once the novel has been read and the students and teachers have engaged in several grand conversations based upon their affective response journals, an interesting postreading activity would be to create new maps of differing binary oppositions. Focusing upon adult-adolescent and life-death binaries and employing examples from the text listed in their journals, ask the students to determine different visuals that map alternative, recursive paths of growth.

These maps would also need to illustrate their nuanced understanding of both how binaries can function and how they can be disrupted, especially through literary interpretations.

For example, students could create a possible path of how a person matures from childhood to adulthood, and along the path would be stops or thresholds that indicate progression. However, the path would not necessarily be linear, and certain thresholds that are traditionally viewed as occurring in adolescence, such as identity formation, could be placed at different moments within both childhood and adulthood. In this way, the maps disrupt the adult-adolescent binary by placing negative associations outside of adolescence and more positive associations within adolescence.

Similarly, students could create visuals of how life and death are related beyond the traditional linear understanding. As Achebe's story indicates, there are cultures that believe the dead live among the living, and are viewed honorably, which also disrupts the life-death binary opposition. Together, these maps and images could easily be used as summative assessments of the novel study to gauge their essential understandings of multiple literacy standards.

CAUTIONS AND ADVICE

As one might imagine, the most controversial aspect of Zevin's (2005) *Elsewhere* lies in its alternative presentation of the afterlife as compared to mainstream religious traditions. The story remains a-religious, and Zevin appears to be careful in not placing any kind of judgment on particular religious traditions, as the story focuses solely on secular and personal issues related to growth and death. Yet, teachers should be careful when choosing such texts about death and dying in order to be sensitive to their students' (and parents') religious beliefs.

Therefore, it is imperative that the teacher be transparent about the underlying curricular and social reasons for choosing this novel. First, begin with getting approval from the administration, as support from the principal will be necessary if any parent attempts to challenge or ban the book from the classroom and the school. Second, send a letter home to parents explaining the curricular and social reasons for choosing *Elsewhere*, relating how Zevin chose to present Liz's death experience, and promising that religious traditions will only be discussed if students question the veracity of the setting due to their own religious beliefs.

Explain that such a discussion would include a statement that Zevin's novel is a piece of fiction, and not meant to present an alternative reality to any religious tradition. Rather, clarify to parents that her story about Liz is meant to spark thought and conversation about how life and death are connected, as well as how growth is not necessarily a linear process. Get permission from parents for their students to read and discuss the book. Of course, it would be necessary to create a curricular plan for students who do not have parent permission as well.

CONCLUSION

The outlined approach for teaching *Elsewhere* presented in this chapter attempts to address the need for cross-generational discussions, or grand conversations, on problematizing binary-based views of both adult-adolescent and life-death relationships. Youth are positioned uniquely to discuss issues related to adolescence—even though teachers and other adults tend to not think of youth from this asset-based perspective—including life and death. Creating an equitable discursive space for such conversations, therefore, treats youth as those with knowledge to share, rather than those that need to be told what to think and believe.

As well, couching the conversations around emotion in the affective response journal allows young readers to attend to how emotional markers indicate that the usual has become strange, and allow someone to consider habit, activities, and beliefs with new information (Nussbaum, 2001). In other words, human understanding is based on emotional understanding, a foundation of well-guided approaches to judgment-making. For example, helping readers to build compassion for Liz's experiences in *Elsewhere* affords more opportunities to (re)consider their understanding about life by making vulnerable judgments about death and dying.

Finally, to reiterate, binary oppositions can be a damaging way to view the world, so providing a literary opportunity to discuss such constructions can be helpful for youth beyond discussions around death education. For example, not only would students see how an adult-adolescent binary privileges adults, they would also deepen their understanding of other binary oppositions, such as life-death, reason-emotion, male-female, and more.

Using *Elsewhere* can be quite fruitful for discussions of binary oppositions with young readers because of how Zevin reverses aging processes, thereby devaluing traditional views of youth and adults. Due to the asset-based perspective of youth on which these instructional tasks rely, it seems that youth would appreciate such an approach to thinking about death and dying, as well as adolescence and adulthood.

BOX 1.1   CONNECTED RESOURCES

Zevin, G. (n.d.). Reading group guide [Blog post]. Retrieved from https://gabriellezevin.com/ya/elsewhere/discussion-questions/

Provides several questions to discuss with *Elsewhere* that expand upon the focus of this chapter.

Miss Parry. (2014, October 1). *Binary oppositions in pride and prejudice* [Video file]. Retrieved from https://www.youtube.com/watch?v=NOXWd48ng44&app=desktop

A video outlining a clear and concise introduction to binary oppositions.

Achebe, C. (1953). Dead men's path. Retrieved from http://www.sabanciuniv.edu/HaberlerDuyurular/Documents/F_Courses_/2012/Dead_Mens_Path.pdf

Provides to a copy of Achebe's short story.

Stephen. (2011, November 21). Dead narrators [Blog post]. Retrieved from https://www.goodreads.com/list/show/14674.Dead_Narrators

Lists other stories with "dead-narrators" that might be paired with *Elsewhere*.

REFERENCES

Bosmajian, H. (2002). *Sparing the child: Grief and the unspeakable in youth literature about Nazism and the holocaust.* New York, NY: Routledge.

Connolly, P. T. (2012). Surviving the storm: Trauma and recovery in children's books about natural disasters. *Bookbird, 50*(1), 1–9.

Harju, M-L. (2009). Encouraging grand conversations: Using crossover picture books to open up new dialogues for death education. *English Quarterly Canada, 39*(2), 17–24.

James, K. (2009). *Death, gender, and sexuality in contemporary adolescent literature.* New York, NY: Routledge.

Lesko, N. (2012). *Act your age! A cultural construction of adolescence* (2nd ed.). New York, NY: Routledge.

Lewis, M. A. (2014). Co-characters in an immigration story: Sixth grade students' narrative interpretations of literature and life. *Middle Grades Research Journal, 9*(1), 19–34.

Nussbaum, M. (2001). *Upheavals of thought: The intelligence of emotions.* New York, NY: Cambridge University Press.

Pytash, K. E. (2013). Using YA literature to help preservice teachers deal with bullying and suicide. *Journal of Adolescent & Adult Literacy, 56* (6), 470–79.

Russell, D. (2015). *Literature for children: A short introduction* (8th ed.). Boston, MA: Pearson.

Stallcup, J. E. (2002). Power, fear, and children's picture books. *Children's Literature, 30*, 125–58.

Šubrtová, M. (2009). When children die in war: Death in war literature for children and youth. *Bookbird, 47*(4), 1–8.

Zevin, G. (2005). *Elsewhere.* New York, NY: Farrar, Straus and Giroux.

Chapter 2

Confronting Death and Mourning in the Liminal through Short Stories

René Saldaña, Jr.

French anthropologist Arnold van Gennep (1960) made his career studying the rites of passage as experienced by various cultures. What he found, ultimately, is that momentous events, such as pregnancy, birth, marriage, and death, signal both passage out of the current phase in a person's life and into the next (p. 10). He observed that each of these events, independently or in combination, fell into one of three categories: they are "*rites of separation, transition rites*, and *rites of incorporation*" (van Gennep, 1960, p. 11, emphasis in original).

In literature, life is usually presented as a series of stages: Shakespeare names seven of them beginning with infancy, culminating in death, which is often the focal point in a work of literature: the "Last scene of all/That ends this strange eventful history/. . . sans everything" (*As You Like It*, trans. 1960b, 2.7. pp. 142–65). There is also, for instance, the tragic end of the "star-crossed lovers" in *Romeo and Juliet*, announced a mere six lines into the play (Prologue, trans. 1960, 6).

Frequently overlooked as central to the story, though, is the mourning by the bereaved and the suffering of their fellow mourners. Again, *Romeo and Juliet* is a perfect example: while patriarchs Montague and Capulet are the logical characters to express their collective sorrow and though present in the final scene, they are cast aside by the Prince who gets the final word: "For never was a story of more woe/Than this of Juliet and her Romeo" (Shakespeare, trans. 1960a, 5.3. pp. 308–9). An anticlimactic ending if ever there was one.

In real life, grieving over loss cannot be so easily disregarded. As a matter of fact, van Gennep (1960) considers this phase as important as the death itself. "During mourning," he writes, "the living mourners and the deceased constitute a special group, situated between the world of the living and the world of the dead" (p. 147), a place that comprises all at once and for all concerned the "rites of entrance, of waiting, and of departure" (van Gennep, 1960, p. 25).

Anthropologist Victor Turner (1992) expounds on van Gennep's (1960) "tripartite processual structure," renaming them "separation; margin (or limen); and reaggregation" (p. 48). The first phase, *separation,* refers to the voluntary or forceful removal of subjects from their everyday lives and or routines for the purpose of enduring a growth ritual, and, after negotiating the *limen, reaggregating* or coming out on the other end "inwardly transformed and outwardly changed" (Turner, 1992, pp. 48–49).

It is the limen that Turner (1992) chooses to concentrate on, the space that he describes as "betwixt and between," where liminaries are "not this or that, here or there, one thing or the other" (p. 49), a place for "thinking hard about the elements and basic building blocks of symbolic complexes they had hitherto taken for granted as 'natural' units" (p. 50).

In its treatment of mourning, contemporary literature does not improve on the old. Death still seems to take center stage while the grieving process is left to be dealt with in the wings. If adolescent readers are meant to learn from literature the ins and outs of a culture by how a character representative of that culture acts and reacts to a variety of situations and events, they don't get much to go on. But, if educators invite their students to look at mourning scenes in fiction, lacking as they may be, through the lens of the limen or threshold, there is much to learn, even if it means learning what not to do or say.

SUMMARIES OF TWO SHORT STORIES

"Tina La Tinaca" by David Rice

David Rice's (2011) "Tina La Tinaca" is the story of Tina Guzmán, who loves her son Héctor more than anything or anyone in this world, and who would do anything for him. She is given the nickname "tinaca," or "water tower," because she is noticeably overweight. At a high school football game one Friday night, she is wearing a gray shirt in support of the hometown team and one boy compares her to the town's water tower (Rice, 2011, p. 65). The name sticks, but she ignores it.

She would rather spend all of her time and love on Héctor, whose dream is to watch his favorite baseball team, the Houston Astros, play in the Astrodome. She makes it happen for him, and together they travel several hours to Houston. They enjoy Astroworld, an amusement park, and the following day they watch the Astros. After the game, Héctor spots their car, "weaving in and out between parked cars." Tragically, he runs "into the path of a slow-moving white truck" (Rice, 2011, p. 69), resulting in his eventual and untimely death.

Tina returns home, but she is not able to recover from the emotional trauma of losing her son. She gives up, in essence, and eventually dies herself.

Instead of sympathizing with her, the townspeople are disgusted by how she let herself and her home go. Julio, one of the Barco brothers earlier charged with bringing back Tina, along with Héctor's corpse, from Houston, mirrors the community's thinking: "This woman was crazy. I mean, look at this house. Parece como una casa de marranos. She didn't care about anything" (Rice, 2011, p. 81). Tina dies sad and alone because ironically she indeed loved with all her heart.

"Finding Our Way" by René Saldaña, Jr.

In "Finding Our Way" (Saldaña, 2015), four life-long friends learn that Danny de los Santos, a boy from school, is found brutally murdered. The news shakes them to their core. Juan, the narrator, grows upset that David, his best friend in the barrio, had tried to befriend Danny without his knowledge. Juan realizes he is more disappointed in himself that he had no idea that David was looking for more depth in their friendship than he was capable of.

Shaken, the friends must still contend with death. One day, David screams at Mando for wanting to talk about Danny: "'Shut up about it!' said David. 'What's the use trying to figure it out? Talk. That's all we do. Talk, talk, and more talk. What good is that?'" (Saldaña, 2015, p. 147). What he doesn't understand is that what Mando needs more than anything is to talk through his own shock. They all could benefit from talking, but they simply do not have the wherewithal.

By the end of their story, they each make their way through the threshold, transformed in their individual ways: "David, Mando, Pete, and I learned something big that summer. I couldn't put it into words then, but I also knew I would not be able to keep quiet when I was ready. I wouldn't whisper anything. I'd have to shout" (Saldaña, 2015, p. 152). But for now, they remain silent. Lamentably, this is the very role students find themselves relegated to play, though it does not have to be.

LIMINALITY AND ROLE-PLAYING TO
LEARN A NEW PART

Prereading: Understanding Rites of Passage

The teacher must first introduce "rites of passage" as the reading approach. To accomplish this, the teacher first explains the concept of "rites of passage." One way to acquaint students with the concept is for the teacher to share his or her own cathartic experience, attaching to each of the stages of that experience van Gennep's (1960) or Turner's (1992) language. This will accomplish two things.

In modeling through sharing, the teacher has made the idea something more tangible. Students can now see separation, transition, and reaggregation. The teacher also sets the tone for the lesson: in this space, the expectation is that students will share similarly (or not), but more importantly, that classmates will give their respect to the speaker. Examples of such cathartic moments include quinceañeras, bar mitzvahs, giving birth, graduation, or leaving home.

Students can then volunteer their own experiences, and they can label the different stages using van Gennep's (1960) or Turner's (1992) language, while the teacher assesses for comprehension of the concept. Once students show understanding, the teacher can shift from real life to "rites of passage" as reading approach.

Teachers can explain that characters in a story undergo their own journeys or rites of passage: they are in the preliminal or separation phase, the middle phase also referred to as the threshold or limen, and the postliminal or reaggregation phase. They are most likely also moving from one stage to the next. Since characters exist in the fictional world, the distance between characters and students permits them to delve more deeply into the character's suffering at loss.

An athlete in a story, for instance, experiences what could be a career-ending injury. This injury forces her from the preliminal into the liminal phase where she will be ground down by this trial, have her mettle tested, where she can reflect on what comes next (Turner, 1992, p. 50). Another character, after hiding in the threshold, mid-transition, reassessing, doing his own reflecting, might exit the threshold after the appropriate length of time to confront a bully.

Readers might allow themselves to feel strongly for these characters, but they are not experiencing their emotional suffering directly. They are detached from it. At this point, the teacher can shift to the topic of death and mourning with less difficulty. It is still only the suffering of fictional characters the students are dealing with.

Journaling about Death and Mourning

The teacher will next introduce the themes of death and mourning as other types of rites of passage. As a prereading activity, students will journal responding to the topic "To me, mourning looks/sounds/smells/feels like. . . ." Teachers want to give their students time to do their own reflection, to gather their thoughts, to come up with their own language with which to start this conversation. In the relative safety of classroom discussion, students will be asked to volunteer to share their journal entries. They will be more apt to contribute to the discussion as they have put their thoughts to paper.

One student may write and share: "To me, mourning smells like soft perfume. I remember standing in line waiting to offer my aunt my condolences after my uncle's death. When I leaned in for a hug and a kiss, she smelled of that perfume." Another might respond thus: "To me, death is the brightness of the sun. And dark sunglasses. I remember standing in the backyard with my cousins waiting to go to the cemetery. Every one of them was wearing dark glasses. I didn't own a pair, so I went without, my face left exposed. Were they looking at me? Could they tell that I didn't know how this kind of sadness was supposed to look on a face?" Yet another, not so prolifically, might write: "Mourning, to me, is the sound of crying."

This first step is important because students need to hear for themselves that on the whole, Western cultures react to death and mourning in very similar ways. Mourners tend to hide behind dark glasses, afraid to speak more than words of pity to the grieving. Anything more is usually out of bounds.

During Reading: Identifying Moments of Grief and Comfort

Once students meet one another as fellow travelers on this journey, they will read the assigned short story through once, pausing only to identify for themselves moments in the piece where the grieving character is desperate for comfort, but the other character(s) offers none, or what he/she does offer falls short. For example, in "Tina La Tinaca" (Rice, 2011), students will recognize such a moment in the following scene: Tina's boy has died only hours before and she finds herself alone in the hospital's waiting room (her liminal space where she is suffering).

The Barco brothers have arrived to drive her and Héctor back home. "When she saw the Barcos walk in, people she knew, people like her, she began to cry." In a quivering voice, she tells them that her son has died. "Julio [Barco] extended his arms to hug and console her, but it was difficult for him to express his emotions. Her body shook in his arms, and he looked over at Joel, who shrugged his shoulders, not knowing what he should do" (Rice, 2011, p. 73).

In "Finding Our Way" (Saldaña, 2015), authorities have not yet reported that Danny de los Santos has been found dead, murdered likely, his corpse horribly dismembered. That will come later in the story for this community. Life-long friends and main characters, Mando, Pete, David, and Juan, at this point in the story believe Danny, a loner at school, has likely run away.

Sitting on buffalo grass in a ditch, one of their barrio hangouts, David, the leader of the group, shares that once he had approached Danny at school. This information surprises Juan because "David doesn't like making new friends"

(Saldaña, 2015, p. 142). It also bothers him that David doesn't think to talk to him "that way, about deep subjects, or stuff that might be embarrassing, like him not liking to read" (Saldaña, 2015, p. 143).

When Danny's death is announced, the friends return to the ditch, this time, though, they are "avoiding the Danny issue" altogether (Saldaña, 2015, p. 147). Left to reflect, Juan thinks that "we were all shaken, thrown off by [the news of Danny's death]. We still had to figure it out for ourselves, especially after there was a report on the news about a guy who was arrested an hour away from us for molesting teen boys" (Saldaña, 2015, p. 147).

Having identified these crucial moments where characters cannot quite offer anything but an awkward embrace or they are avoiding the subject of death, students will be assigned to small groups wherein they will first discuss where the Barco brothers failed to give the grief-stricken mother the emotional support she desperately needs, and how the four life-long friends could have supported one another by talking through their torment.

Postreading: Composing Skits and Role-Playing

Next, students will work out an alternative to the aforementioned behaviors. They will begin by asking themselves, "What could the Barco brothers have done differently that would have given Tina the comfort she needed at that moment?" Students might argue that what they should have done was to offer her the embrace of someone who knows about loss because, after all, haven't the Barco brothers also lost a loved one, too, a grandmother maybe, or a cousin? The next question is, "Now, what does that alternative look and sound like?" Based on this back and forth, students will then compose their skits.

Finally, they will role-play this alternative in front of classmates, who will in turn watch and listen to this presentation. Their task now is to consider this alternative and to be ready to react to it. The teacher could prompt them with the following: "Is this a realistic way of dealing with another person's suffering?" "Can you offer your own alternative?" and "How is this alternative response more helpful to the grieving and to the comforter?"

Students may not realize that they have stepped into a liminal space of their own. The moment they got into groups, they separated themselves from their individual understanding of death and mourning, stepped into the threshold, and began "thinking hard about the elements and basic building blocks of symbolic complexes they had hitherto taken for granted as 'natural' units" (Turner, 1992, p. 50), thus challenging their traditional roles when faced with death and mourning. The teacher can point this out after the fact and in this way teach them that this is another critical approach to reading: to study a work of fiction from inside the threshold.

Turner (1992) writes that "parts of liminality may be given over to experimental behavior" during which students may "discover something not yet known" (p. 52) about themselves or the subject at hand. He adds, "In liminality, new ways of acting, new combinations of symbols, are tried out, to be discarded or accepted" (p. 52). Students/liminaries are not constrained by society's expectations of them; instead, within the threshold, they are free to act another's part.

When students experiment with alternative reactions to death and mourning by acting them out, they are experiencing "*freedom to* transcend social-structural normative limitations, the freedom to *play*—with ideas, with fantasies, with words" (Turner, 1992, p. 54, emphasis in original). Said differently, they have the permission to respond to death and mourning unlike they normally would or are expected to do in their own lives.

CAUTIONS AND ADVICE

Though not as popular a form to use in the reading/literature classroom as the novel, the short story's compact nature makes it the ideal form to complete the work described in this chapter. Authentic reading and writing time in the classroom is in direct competition against standardized testing. Teachers find themselves having to teach the usual content plus more, and so time becomes more and more limited. Using short fiction will permit teachers to teach the content (genre/form, point of view, character development, etc.) and approach literature in a real life and useful way: students have all suffered loss, and they all need to learn how to deal with it.

Another word of caution. Some students may not participate the way teachers would expect them to have taken every reasonable caution. Although there are a variety of reasons why students may not participate like teachers hope, it is preferable, even advantageous for the teacher and the project's success to err on the side of caution. Perhaps these students are too close to the topic that active participation in such a project might further traumatize them. Instead, consider redefining "participation." Van Gennep (1960) writes, "During mourning, social [and learning] life is suspended for all those affected by it" (p. 148).

If, indeed, students are grieving, it is not that they are not participating; quite the contrary: they are in the threshold reassessing, reflecting; they are mid-transition. Vicariously, then, watching and listening to classmates perform their skits they are doing some hard thinking of their own, reformulating "the elements and basic building blocks of symbolic complexes they had hitherto taken for granted as 'natural' units" (Turner, 1992, p. 50). Respect that space. Validate their attempt to regroup in the between and betwixt (Turner, 1992, p. 49).

CONCLUSION

Often, it is much more convenient to get in line with fellow mourners to offer the bereaved condolences. "I'm sorry for your loss," they will say. They will also tender a hug, and then be on their way having fulfilled their duties as fellow mourners. But this is not enough. It matters that they reach out in this moment of sorrow, to try as they might to shoulder some of the bereft's emotional weight, if even for a moment. Words and a warm embrace, though appreciated, are not sufficient. Sometimes taking time to cry with the bereaved means more.

Regrettably, the treatment of mourning for the dead has not changed much since the time of the Montagues and the Capulets. Today's literature doesn't quite teach adolescent readers how to respond to sorrow either. Death still plays the central role in a story. Grieving and buttressing the bereft are dealt with offstage, for the most part.

Educators can make a difference. They can provide students the language of grieving and empathizing with the mourner through the use of literature, and in particular by having students, through journaling, small group discussions, sharing, and role-playing, experiment with a variety of possible alternative behaviors that are not the norm in hopes that they will "discover something not yet known" (Turner, 1992, p. 52).

REFERENCES

Rice, D. (2011). Tina la tinaca. In *Heart-shaped cookies and other stories* (pp. 65–82). Tempe, AZ: Bilingual Press/Editorial Bilingüe.

Saldaña, R. Jr. (2015). Finding our way. In *Heartbeat of the soul of the world* (pp. 133–52). Donna, TX: Juventud Press.

Shakespeare, W. (1960a). *Romeo and Juliet*. P. Alexander, Ed. London: Collins.

Shakespeare, W. (1960b). *As you like it*. P. Alexander, Ed. London: Collins.

Turner, V. (1992). *Blazing the trail: Way marks in the exploration of symbols* (E. Turner, ed.). Tucson, AZ: The University of Arizona Press.

van Gennep, A. (1960). *The rites of passage* (M.B. Vizedom & G. L. Caffee, Trans.). Chicago, IL: University of Chicago Press.

BOX 2.1   CONNECTED RESOURCES

Brooks, G. (2017). *We real cool* [Video file]. Retrieved from https://www.poetryfoundation.org/video/142394/we-real-cool

> Though a poem, this is the tragic story of teens whose lives end tragically, though mundanely. The video format offers an extended, musical, and visual narrative that the poem by itself does not. Students can invent the parts of the pool players as they are not named nor numbered. Each player will have his own reason for heading down this fatal path, the skit allowing students an opportunity to step out of themselves to speak frankly about the players' thoughts on their eventual death.

Reynolds, J. (2017). *Long way down*. New York, NY: Atheneum.

> Written in the form of poetry, this novel is a quick read and suitable for this project. Will Holloman, the narrator, is on his way to seek revenge for his brother's murder. On the elevator down, he meets a new ghost from his past at every floor, who doles out otherworldly wisdom about gun violence and vengeance. Students can play the ghosts, but instead of offering guidance from beyond, they can let themselves go emotionally, inviting the ghosts to speak about who and what they left behind.

Woodson, J. (2017). Main street. In E. Oh (Ed.) *Flying lessons & other stories*. New York, NY: Crown.

> Though the main character is young, she speaks beautifully to the subject of a child's voicelessness during the mourning process. The girl's father dismisses her feelings, stating that as a child she could not possibly know pain. Students, each playing the girl, could come up with one way that they feel pain at her mother's passing and in a circle "speak their pain" to the person playing the father who is standing in the middle of the mourning circle.

Chapter 3

Mourning a Missing Generation: Using *Pedro and Me* to Teach the AIDS Epidemic and to ACT UP in ELA Classrooms

James Joshua Coleman

How does one mourn the death of a generation? For the queer community, the need to mourn persists in the wake of the AIDS epidemic of the 1980s and 1990s. We look for them, yet their absence is glaring. They are the "Missing Generation."

Forsaken by a government sworn to protect them, gay men became the primary victims of the AIDS epidemic. Originally named "gay-related immune deficient" (GRID) by medical professionals, AIDS soon gathered social recognition, being referred to as the "gay plague." Inciting social panic, AIDS-related deaths became a means to mobilize politics for the queer community, while for the U.S. government, it remained little more than a source of silence and laughter.

On October 15, 1982, in a harrowing interview with the White House press secretary, echoes of laughter resounded from the press corps and Deputy Press Secretary Larry Speaks as Journalist Rev. Lester Kingsolver inquired as to President Ronald Reagan's knowledge of "A-I-D-S," at the time an "epidemic [with] over 600 cases" (Lawson, 2015). Reagan remained silent on the subject of AIDS for an additional three years, until the death toll had risen to over 5,000.

By 1993—the height of the AIDS epidemic in the United States—over 234,000 individuals had passed away from AIDS, most of whom identified as gay men. Deemed the Missing Generation, these men were lost to this world, their bodies allowed to wither away by a government that refused to see them. Beyond the loss of their bodies, so too are their histories missing, unheard in U.S. classrooms.

A community ravaged by plague, the plague of homophobia, one must ask: Why this generation of missing gay men continues to be absent from English language arts (ELA) classrooms and curricula? Why does the author, as a twenty-seven-year-old gay man, only now learn of the history of his community? Of the gruesome deaths of hundreds of thousands of gay men whose stories deserve, no need, to be told? Accordingly, this chapter proposes a user guide for ELA teachers to make visible this Missing Generation, by educating about the activism of the past in order to champion those living with HIV and AIDS today.

Promoting AIDS education, this chapter provides teachers with skills in multimodal literary analysis (MLA) as well as the historical knowledge necessary to help students ACT UP (AIDS Coalition to Unleash Power). Propelled by this coalition's mantra "Silence=Death" (Royles, 2016), this chapter will first introduce "Prereading" vocabulary necessary for conducting MLA.

The author then provides guided and independent practice opportunities based on two images related to AIDS activism: Keith Haring's *Ignorance = Fear* and the Gran Fury poster *Kissing Doesn't Kill*. Finally, to build historical knowledge, this "Prereading" section will provide a brief history of ACT UP, an AIDS activist organization associated with both aforementioned images.

The "During Reading" section of the chapter demonstrates how teachers might support students conduct an MLA of Judd Winick's (2000) intimate graphic memoir, *Pedro & Me: Friendship, Loss, & What I Learned* (2000). Finally, in "Postreading," this chapter will teach students to ACT UP. Choosing an issue important to them, students will engage in technological writing by creating research-based political posters, which will then be presented to the class.

SUMMARY OF *PEDRO AND ME: FRIENDSHIP, LOSS, & WHAT I LEARNED*

A Robert F. Silbert award winner for Children's and Young Adult Literature and American Library Association Notable Children's Book, Judd Winick's (2000) graphic memoir *Pedro & Me: Friendship, Loss & What I Learned* is more than a narrative about living with HIV; it is an elegy to a friend and activist whose life was spent combating silence and ignorance regarding AIDS education and activism. Winick's (2000) beautifully composed graphic text shares the intimate details of how his experiences on a reality show radically altered the trajectory of his life by forming a friendship that continued beyond death.

The memoir unfolds around Winick's selection to join the cast of *The Real World: San Francisco*, a reality television show whose drama unfolds—according to the tagline of the show—"when people stop being polite . . . and start getting real." While the show's drama typically originates from interpersonal conflict, Winick's conflict instead begins internally when he learns he will be "living with someone who has AIDS" (Winick, 2000, p. 22)—a misperception quickly proven false when Pedro shares his HIV+ status.

Intimate and vulnerable, the remainder of this memoir expounds upon Winick's internal struggle to understand HIV and AIDS education by confronting the guilt he has as a "liberal" man scared to live with someone HIV+, the fear that surfaces when he learns that that man is his roommate, and the pain of losing a friend who has changed the course of his life.

Beyond Winick's (2000) personal story, *Pedro and Me* provides a portrait of Pedro Zamora, an HIV+ man of color, whose legacy of AIDS activism and education has extended far beyond his short life. Braiding together Winick's own educational history with Pedro's life story, this graphic memoir combines verbal and visual textual modes to call attention to the failure of schools and media to educate accurately about HIV contraction and living with HIV/AIDS.

Pedro & Me, a kaleidoscope of word and image, furthers Pedro's legacy by combining personal narrative with anecdote and oral histories in a manner appropriate for both young people and adults. The novel provides a face—the face of Pedro Zamora—to humanize the grueling death statistics of the 1980s and 1990s and concomitant representations of AIDS in media.

CULTIVATING MULTIMODAL LITERARY ANALYSIS THROUGH PRE, DURING, AND POSTREADING STRATEGIES

To engage with *Pedro and Me*, this section will be structured according to "Pre," "During," and "Postreading" strategies. "Prereading" strategies are intended to activate prior knowledge and build a framework for engaging with the primary themes of a text. "During Reading" is intended to hone close-reading skills and specific methods of analysis that prepare students to engage in robust discussion of textual themes. "Postreading" provides students an opportunity to reflect on their learning and to practice skills through some culminating product.

Together, these "Pre," "During," and "Postreading" strategies demonstrate how visual and literary texts about the AIDS epidemic address ELA standards that demand the use of textual evidence in support of high-level inferences, analysis across textual modes, comprehension of authorial choice, and the use of technology to craft a written argument.

Prereading

Multimodal Literary Analysis

In preparation for reading graphic texts such as *Pedro and Me*, students must hone skills with visual analysis. While many traditional novels are written in a single mode (verbal), increasingly young adult literature is being composed in multimodal forms, such as comic books, graphic novels, and graphic memoirs. Students need to build competency in combining traditional literary analysis with visual analysis—the analyzing of images—in order to conduct MLA.

Accordingly, in preparation for *Pedro & Me*, teachers can have students practice visual analysis on two images connected to the primary theme of the text: queer activism as resistance to silence about AIDS. Those images are *Ignorance = Fear* (figure 3.1) and *Kissing Doesn't Kill* (figure 3.2). Copies of both images are easily found through Internet searches.

Teachers should begin teaching visual analysis by giving no context for the image and by covering up all verbal text on figure 3.1 (*Ignorance = Fear*) except for the title. By covering up the words, students will be forced to focus on the visual elements of the image. The teacher should then model for

Figure 3.1.   Ignorance = Fear by Keith Haring, 1989; Keith Haring artwork © Keith Haring Foundation

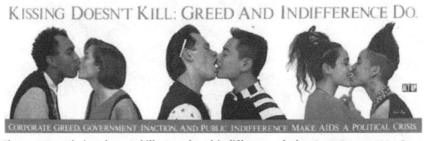

Figure 3.2.   Kissing doesn't kill: Greed and indifference do by Gran Fury, 1989; Gran Fury Collection, Manuscripts and Archives Division, The New York Public Library

students how to analyze key visual elements such as color, style, and form for potential meaning. A teacher think-aloud might sound something like this:

> *When I look at this image, I am struck first by the colors of the image. Red, Blue, and Yellow are primary colors and thus reinforce the rudimentary style, calling forward a sort of primitivism[1] or back-to-basics idea. I'm not sure what this means, but it makes me consider the "see no evil, hear no evil, and speak no evil" theme portrayed by the three forms in a new light. Associated with the maxim of the "Three wise monkeys," I wonder if this connects with the primitive style of the image?*
>
> *It seems however that the conventional wisdom of that maxim—to stay away from "evil"—is being inverted in this image as all three human forms are covered with a pink X. The color pink strikes me as different from the primary colors; maybe this is connected to some specific history or community? The pink triangle at the bottom of the image makes me think about the holocaust because I know that "homosexuals"[2] were often labeled with a pink triangle. So maybe this piece has something do to with the queer community and the death that comes from refusing to see, hear, and speak about evil enacted against them?*

Following the think-aloud, teachers should then invite students to build upon this analysis. Ask students to share their own inferences and to support their analysis by providing visual evidence based on color, style, and form. Conclude analyzing this image by asking students to fill in the covered up verbal texts and inquire, *how would you caption the covered-up sections of this image and why? What do you think the original captions are and why?*

Next in small groups, provide students with a copy of figure 3.2, *Kissing Doesn't Kill*, covering up all verbal text except for the title. Have students conduct a visual analysis based on those key elements of color, style, and form. If need be, students might use a simple graphic organizer such as the one located in table 3.1. Concluding this activity, lead a whole group share-out and then explain to students that these posters are political posters connected to a specific historical moment in U.S. history and that, at the end of the lesson, students will be asked to make a poster of their own for a cause they believe in.

Table 3.1. Graphic Organizer for Visual Analysis

Visual Element	Evidence	Analysis
Color		
Style		
Form		
Synthesis:		

ACT UP

Standing for the AIDS coalition to Unleash Power, ACT UP is an activist organization formed in 1987 in response to failures by the U.S. government to provide for queer individuals living with AIDS (Westervelt, 2017). Practicing civil disobedience, ACT UP, now thirty years old, remains an intergenerational organization consisting primarily of queer[3] individuals. Embracing the slogan "Silence = Death," ACT UP operates according to the belief that "there is tremendous power in smaller actions that can reverberate in unexpected ways" (Westervelt, 2017).

To introduce this topic to students, teachers might play the trailer to *United in Anger: A History of ACT UP* (Hubbard, 2012). Framing the trailer, ask students to share what comes to their minds when they hear the word AIDS.

Following a brief discussion and the creation of a concept web, inform students that in the 1980s and 1990s an epidemic took place in the United States; the AIDS epidemic impacted primarily the queer community and was ignored for years by the U.S. government (see box 3.1 for more information). Now play the trailer *United in Anger* and ask students to consider the following question: *What is ACT UP? Why was the organization created? What does activism mean and look like for this organization?*

Following a brief discussion, explain that the two political posters analyzed at the beginning of the lesson were both created for ACT UP and reveal to students the previously concealed text found on those posters. Finally, in two groups, ask students to reinterpret the posters in light of what they now know about ACT UP and the history of the AIDS epidemic. Discuss with the whole class and explain that this historical information will provide background for the primary text for this unit, *Pedro and Me: friendship, Loss, & What I Learned.*

Teaching Graphic Texts

In the final prereading preparation for *Pedro and Me*, students must learn specific vocabulary for combining visual and verbal analysis into MLA for graphic texts. For students new to graphic texts, terms such as panel, gutters, sequencing, speech bubbles, and caption provide a crucial set of tools for engaging in MLA and without them analyzing graphic memoirs can be frustrating.

Based on the definitions provided in table 3.2, teachers should explain each of the key terms—panel, gutters, sequencing, speech bubbles, and caption—to students (for additional support turn to box 3.1). Then have students work in small groups to paraphrase each of the definitions. Teachers should then check for understanding by having students share-out their paraphrases.

Table 3.2.   Definitions of Graphic Text Terms

Term	Panel	Gutters	Sequencing	Speech Bubble	Caption
Definition	Refers to the framed image. Provides the reader a point of view on the subject sometimes referred to as camera angle. Sometimes panels do not have borders.	The space between panels. Often action the reader does not see occurs here.	The order and layout of panels. Sequencing conveys the action of the plot.	Often circular in shape, these are spaces for character dialogue.	Generally rectangular, these are spaces for narration.

Finally, teachers should work with students to apply these terms to a high-interest section of *Pedro & Me*; pages 24–25 provide a powerful example that provokes interest, previews the content of the book, and demonstrates Winick's (2000) unique authorial choices made to combat deleterious representations of individuals living with AIDS.

During Reading

As MLA will be new for most students, the "During Reading" section of this chapter will focus on close-reading practices of a sequence of panels. This section will provide teachers with the confidence to instruct students on using MLA when reading longer graphic texts, such as graphic memoirs or novels, and will help students develop skills in working across mediums and modes. Note that while the example provided focuses on a sequence of panels, some students might begin by analyzing a single panel. (For additional support using graphic text terminology, please refer to box 3.1.)

To begin instruction on MLA, teachers should provide students with a guiding question to focus their analysis; this question typically connects to the themes of both the unit and text and addresses ELA standards such as what choices an author makes to construct an argument across a text. For *Pedro & Me*, one such guiding question might be: *How does Winick's graphic memoir use verbal and visual textual elements to further AIDS education and/or activism?*

To support gradual release of responsibility, teachers might use an "I do, we do, you do" format to both introduce and demonstrate MLA for students. Weaving together the vocabulary learned for visual analysis and graphic texts with more traditional literary analysis, teachers can use the graphic organizer in table 3.3 to guide the "I Do" or teacher-lead portion of introducing MLA.

Addressing the guiding question, teachers might begin by analyzing the sequence of panels on page 5. Teachers should think-aloud their MLA of the text, while filling in the table 3.3 graphic organizer on the board; they might say: "I first noticed in the upper left-hand panel that Pedro is positioned in the center; this indicates his importance. Also, the black and white style draws my attention to him. I then see the words 'Pedro was a nationally recognized AIDS educator and activist.' This reinforces his importance: he is positioned centrally within the panel and is described verbally as a 'national' figure.

I then notice in the caption underneath the second row of panels, 'He became an international face of AIDS. That face was one of strength, compassion, and sensitive.' I also notice that Pedro is featured five times, once in each panel on the page. Combining modes, Winick demonstrates Pedro's importance to the world by depicting him both visually and verbally as strong, compassionate, and sensitive. Winick's text humanizes those living with AIDS, by giving it a face; it simultaneously builds empathy in the reader and a desire to learn more."

Once completing this first example of MLA and responding to questions, teachers should then transition to the "We do" section of "During Reading" so students can begin practicing MLA with support. In the "We do" portion, teachers continue to support students heavily but allow them to drive the process. Choosing another sequence of panels from *Pedro & Me*, students should work with a teacher to fill in a second table 3.1 graphic organizer. This is a great time for students to make mistakes, as teachers are present to correct misunderstandings.

Table 3.3. Graphic Organizer for Multimodal Literary Analysis

Guiding Question: How does Winick's graphic memoir use verbal and visual textual elements to further AIDS education and activism?

Verbal Evidence	*Visual Evidence*
- "Pedro was a nationally recognized AIDS educator and activist" (p. 5). - "He became an international face of AIDS. That face was one of strength, compassion, and sensitive" (p. 5).	- First Panel: Pedro is positioned in the center of the panel. - Page 5: Pedro is depicted in five panels in several ways: friend, lover, kind, pensive, smiling, relaxed, animated.

Multimodal Analysis:

Winick's text invokes the genre of graphic memoir to emphasize both Pedro's personal importance as a friend and his importance as an AIDS educator and activist. Winick emphasizes this dual importance by depicting Pedro multiple times on the same page and positioning him in the center of each panel. Portrayed as a friend, lover, pensive, smiling, relaxed, and animated, Pedro becomes a complex character that transforms the "international face of AIDS." A real human, who displays strength, compassion, and sensitivity, Pedro demands that readers reconsider AIDS in light of Winick's humanizing work.

Finally, transitioning to "You Do," students whether individually or in groups should practice MLA on their own; they may continue to use the graphic organizer if desired. Teachers might scaffold for students by choosing sections of analysis for them. Concluding this "During Reading" section, engage the class in a whole-group discussion using the following discussion questions:

- What does Winick's graphic memoir teach about AIDS and those living with it?
- What sequence of panels impacted your impression of AIDS the most and why? What visual and verbal components of those panels lead to this impact?
- How would you redesign a panel or sequence of panels to enhance the novels address of AIDS education and activism?
- Do you feel that graphic memoir was the appropriate genre for Winick to further Pedro's life mission? How does Winick's characterization of Pedro impact your response?

Postreading

To reinforce the skills in MLA and to address ELA standards regarding the use of technology to construct an argument, students will conclude this lesson by creating a political poster of their own. Using the ACT UP posters *Ignorance = Fear* and *Kissing Doesn't Kill* as guides, students should create a political poster that connects to some issue of personal importance. Students should conduct research on their chosen topic and generate a slogan (e.g., "Silence=Death") and a symbol (e.g., the pink triangle) to encapsulate the political climate surrounding their issue and to advocate for their chosen community.

Students should approach the poster from a multimodal perspective and be capable of justifying both their visual and verbal choices. Some students may feel more comfortable creating their poster using a collage-style approach first; accordingly, teachers might provide poster paper, used newspapers and magazines, and coloring utensils. Ultimately, students should use digital tools for their creation. Canva.com provides one useful online platform for creating posters. With easy-to-use tutorials, this digital platform will aid almost any student in creating professional-looking poster projects.

To share their work, students might present their poster orally, while students in the audience should prepare questions that address the artist's multimodal choices. Some examples include the following:

- What do your color choices mean?
- Why did you include __(insert a visual or verbal element of poster)__?
- How does _(insert visual element of poster)_ reinforce the meaning of your slogan?

Finally, depending on administration or district expectation, teachers might assign an explanatory or reflective essay for students to explicate their verbal and visual choices; they can share research on their chosen issues and community as well as justify how their poster advocates for their political cause. This essay might explain how their poster relates to activism and provide clarity on how that activism helped them master ELA standards regarding high-level inferences, multimodal analysis, authorial choice, and writing with technology.

CAUTIONS AND ADVICE

First and foremost, teaching about the AIDS epidemic and the Missing Generation takes bravery and courage; it takes individuals impassioned by social justice and the need to bring to light the oft hidden histories of marginalized communities. That being said, this work also demands an educationally and politically supportive environment, an administration and district willing to support brave choices in the classroom.

When teaching about topics connected to sexuality, teachers must be attuned to school, community, and district climates and make wise choices regarding the presentation of this material. For example, districts with abstinence-only sex education might turn to organizations such as the American Library Association and GLSEN (Gay, Lesbian, and Straight Education Network) for support in introducing such material.

Teachers should watch and read all material fully, deciding which sections are appropriate for their students. Finally, it is important to fight against the continued erasure of this community. Be Bold. Be Brave. Bring light to this seldom remembered history, to the AIDS epidemic, and to the Missing Generation.

CONCLUSION

The final page of *Pedro & Me* concludes with the words, "We Honor Those We Love by Remembering Them" (Winick, 2000, p. 180). To teach the history of the AIDS epidemic through young adult literature is an act of remembering, of honoring the lives of that Missing Generation of queer individuals. Accordingly, humanizing the face of AIDS, Pedro Zamora's story presents a powerful opportunity to propel AIDS education and activism, by dispelling misconceptions surrounding AIDS and promoting activism and the drive to ACT UP. It is time that the Missing Generation was honored, by remembering their stories in ELA classrooms across America.

BOX 3.1 CONNECTED RESOURCES

Royles, D. S. (2016, October). Silence = death: It's time to teach AIDS history. *Perspectives on History: The Newsmagazine of the American Historical Association.* Retrieved from https://www. historians.org/publications-and-directories/perspectives-on-history/october-2016/silence-death-its-time-to-teach-aids-history

> Distributed by the American History Association, this article provides a historical overview of the AIDS epidemic as well as additional teaching resources (e.g., primary resources, documentaries, and books).

Hubbard, J., & Schulman, S. (n.d.). United in anger: A history of ACT UP. Retrieved from http://www.unitedinanger.com/

> This website supports the documentary *United by Anger: A History of ACT UP* providing both activist guides and a study guide.

ACT UP Oral History Project. (n.d.). Interviews. Retrieved from http://www.actuporalhistory.org/interviews/index.html

> This oral history project catalogues hundreds of interviews with ACT UP participants, providing primary source documentation of the organization's workings.

Mcintyre, D., & Pruzinsky, T. (n.d.). Graphic novel. Retrieved from https://www.thinkib.net/englishalanglit/page/13891/graphic-novel

> Geared toward IB English, this resource provides a useful introduction to basic terms for analyzing graphic novels.

Scholastic. (2005). A guide to using graphic novels with children and teens. Retrieved from https://www.scholastic.com/graphix_teacher/pdf/Graphix%20Teachers%20guide.pdf

> A comprehensive teacher's guide from scholastic for teaching and recommending graphic novels.

NOTES

1. An art-specific term, "primitivism" in this sense refers only to the style of art-work; its usage is not intended to connote more pejorative meanings often associated with the term primitive.

2. The use of "homosexuals" reflects terminology deployed during the Holocaust to describe individuals persecuted for same-sex attraction. Homosexual was origi-nally a medical term coined in the late nineteenth century and, for many, still carries with it pathologizing connotations.

3. Queer in this instance refers most directly to LGBT+ identified people. How-ever, queer can also be an antinormative way of being that, while commonly aligned with LGBT+ identification, might also include opposite-sex attracted individuals, those who identify fluidly, or those who do not identify as any sexual identity.

REFERENCES

ACT UP Oral History Project. (n.d.). Interviews. Retrieved from http://www.actupor alhistory.org/interviews/index.html

Hubbard, J. (2012). United in anger trailer. Retrieved from http://www.unitedinanger. com/?page_id=158

Lawson, R. (2015, December 1). The Reagan administration's unearthed responses to the AIDS crisis is chilling: A new short film, *When AIDS Was Funny*, unearths never-before-heard audio reaction to the escalating AIDS crisis. *Vanity Fair*. Retrieved from https://www.vanityfair.com/news/2015/11/ reagan-administration-response-to-aids-crisis

Royles, D. (2016, October). Silence = death: It's time to teach AIDS history. *Perspectives on History: The Newsmagazine of the American Historical Asso-ciation*. Retrieved from https://www.historians.org/publications-and-directories/ perspectives-on-history/october-2016/silence-death-its-time-to-teach-aids-history

Westervelt, E. (Host). (2017, April 17). ACT UP at 30: Reinvigorated for Trump fight. [Radio Broadcast Episode] *NPR*. https://www.npr.org/2017/04/17/522726303/ act-up-at-30-reinvigorated-for-trump-fight

Winick, J. (2000). *Pedro and me: Friendship, loss, and what I learned*. New York, NY: Square Fish Books.

Part II

MURDER

Chapter 4

When It Feels Like Death, but It Ain't: Spirit-Murder in *All American Boys*

Stephanie P. Jones

Any educator who has spent time reading and teaching literature will recognize the significance of death and dying as part of the literary tradition. Even the readers in our classrooms will engage in discussions about death—from the foreshadowed fate of Romeo and Juliet to the unforgiving death of Tom in *To Kill a Mockingbird*. Yet, as much as death generates dialogue, both in and outside of our classrooms, our conversations are, for the most part, limited to literal death and its symbolism and significance. This chapter is also about death. But not about the type of death teachers may be accustomed to teaching.

Approaching this topic in the classroom is embedded with using and teaching through a lens of criticality. Discussions about death and more specifically a certain type of death caused by the impact of racism assume working within an anti-racist pedagogy, which is described subsequently in this chapter. This form of pedagogy makes room for discussions about not only the existence of systemic racism but also how this system impacts those who are suffering from its effect.

This chapter explores spirit-murder (Williams, 1991), a form of repetitive and emotional death caused by the impact of racism. Using excerpts from the novel, *All American Boys*, this chapter explores how teachers can create curricula that engages students in discussions about the physical, mental, and emotional toll that death and spirit-murder does to characters within young adult literature and in life.

SUMMARY OF *ALL AMERICAN BOYS*

In 2013, George Zimmerman was acquitted of the murder of Trayvon Martin, a black unarmed teenager. As a response to their shared frustration over brutality against innocent black bodies, authors Brendan Kiely and Jason Reynolds (2015) coauthored *All American Boys*, a story of two teenagers whose lives become deeply intertwined through an act of violence.

The story centers around teens Rashad Butler and Quinn Collins. Rashad, a black teenager who is wrongly accused of shoplifting in a convenience store, is brutally beaten by a white police officer, Paul Galluzzo. While Rashad is shopping for chips at a neighborhood convenient store, he mistakenly falls into a white woman patron at the store. Soon after, Galluzzo approaches Rashad and accuses him of theft and assault. As Rashad attempts to explain that he was not stealing anything, Galluzzo interprets Rashad's defense as aggressive and resisting arrest. Galluzzo then proceeds to assault Rashad to the point of hospitalization.

Not only was the incident filmed, but Quinn, another high school student who is white, witnesses the violent act and soon learns that the cop is his best friend's brother. Both Rashad and Quinn struggle with the aftermath of the beating. Rashad attempts to make sense of the physical and emotional brutality of violence and its toll on his family and friends. Quinn's loyalty is divided between being a witness to an act of police brutality of an innocent black teenager at the hands of an officer and that this officer is close family friend.

The racial identities of the both the authors and main characters of *All American Boys* are significant in that future discussions of issues like silence, racial profiling, and spirit-murder are enmeshed in how teachers learn to teach stories like *All American Boys*.

TEACHING CRITICALLY ABOUT DEATH AND VIOLENCE

It is perhaps not surprising that in order to teach critically about death and violence using *All American Boys*, that teachers should have an understanding of the historical context and current climate of violence against black bodies, especially when their own students may encounter this form of trauma inside and outside of school spaces. When it comes to formal educational contexts, engaging in a discussion about spirit-murder must be accompanied by an anti-racist framework and pedagogy.

To help explain this framework, this chapter will be organized around a series of questions. The rationale for organizing this framework around a series of questions has multiple, necessary meanings.

First, engaging a concept like spirit-murder requires that teachers consider how racism is embedded in the plot and the subsequent impact on Rashad and Quinn. The instructional goal of teaching *All American Boys* should include both teachers and students creating, asking, and answering questions that model an anti-racist framework and leads to a deeper understanding of death in young adult literature.

Second, moving beyond plot summary and comprehension questions suggests that critical questions should be the driving force in curriculum design. Moving from conceptual to practical, these questions initially foreground the concepts needed to teach with *All American Boys* and then help to facilitate ways of engaging with the text that moves beyond plot summary.

Third, organizing around a series of questions helps to frame these ideas into activities that engage students' prior knowledge around spirit-death and additionally help to foster ideas for how to work with students during and after the reading of *All American Boys*. The ideas in this chapter are best implemented within the structure and pedagogy of an anti-racist classroom. In order to achieve this, teachers should consider what activities would align with this framework while including a teach-in of what an anti-racist pedagogy looks and sounds like.

What Is an Anti-Racist Pedagogy?

The current educational buzz words include such terms as diverse, multicultural, and inclusion. Part of the conversations surrounding these concepts is the desire for teachers to make their classrooms a space where all voices and identities are welcomed and are part of the curriculum. An anti-racist framework takes up these same ideals while also expanding to consider how racism is integrated in the education process. As a foundation, there are certain tenets that encompass an anti-racist framework (Galliers, 1987). They include

- racism exists, and it is structural and institutional,
- racism is defined by its effect and not its intent,
- racism is a learned behavior and can be unlearned, and
- racism can be dismantled through individual and collective action.

For anti-racist educators, the task is to think about how the texts teachers use to engage our students, either address or ignore these tenets, and in what ways can teachers ask students to participate in work that challenges their perceptions of race and racism.

What Is Spirit-Murder?

Legal scholar Patricia Williams (1991) defines spirit-murder as a form of racism that causes personal, psychological, and spiritual injury. The residual impact of racism is often invisible, and spirit-murder is continuously nurtured through an unwillingness to acknowledge the existence of racism, its relationship to the legacy of slavery, and its connections to privilege and power. Thus, dying in the context of spirit-murder is a repeated occurrence often resulting in the denial of "inclusion, protection, safety, nurturance, and acceptance" (Love, 2014, p. 302) for its victims.

It is important to distinguish here that spirit-murder, according to Williams (1991), happens as part of the victims' experience with being viewed as an "object." In particular, spirit-murder dehumanizes its victim through verbal and physical actions, regardless if the intention of those actions was to do no harm.

There are numerous examples of spirit-murder occurring within literature and within the school environments for black and brown children. In literature, these examples span across genres and time periods. From Sethe in *Beloved* to Frederick Douglass to Martin Luther King to the nameless protagonist in *Invisible Man*, the impact of dehumanizing racism is present. In schools, these examples range from Ahmed Mohamed, a fourteen-year-old student from Texas, arrested for bringing a clock to school, to an unnamed black girl thrown from her desk by a school resource officer for not following her teacher's instructions (Pearce & Thomas, 2015).

Given these examples, finding instances of spirit-murder in literature and beyond is not a difficult task. Situating these occurrences as part of a unit on spirit-murder means that examples from both literature and recent news accounts can be used to coconstruct knowledge about this term within an anti-racist space. Part of our responsibility as teachers is to continue to have discussions about difficult topics by constantly expanding what it means to think about death in literature.

The Impact of Spirit-Murder: Those Who Experience It and Its Connection to Racialized Trauma

The impact of spirit-murder is what makes this phenomenon different from experiencing a literal death between the pages of a text. Spirit-murder is a by-product of racism, and accordingly, they share the same characteristics. Constant stress caused by dehumanizing words, actions, and policies result in symptoms such as "depression, generalized anxiety, low self-esteem, flashbacks, difficulty concentrating, irritability, and jumpiness" (Williams & Leins, 2016, p. 32). Essentially, race-based traumas and spirit-murder has the same mental health impact as those suffering from post-traumatic stress disorder.

Teaching from within an anti-racist framework demands that teachers problematize and confront the saliency of how death is discussed in the classroom. Educators can position themselves better by thinking about how racial acts can be both silent and innocuous, and still have significant and deadly impacts.

Prereading: How Can I Teach about Spirit-Murder Using *All American Boys*?

In an anti-racist English language arts classroom, teachers should provide learning opportunities for their students to read deeply while writing for multiple purposes. The topic of spirit-murder is not an easy undertaking but deciding to teach this powerful concept is a challenge that teachers should undertake. These ideas are inspired by a question posed by English education scholar, Maisha Winn. She asked, "How do we teach in a way that makes people stop killing?" (Winn, 2016). An anti-racist pedagogy demands that teachers use the literature at our disposal to question how certain structures continue to exist and cause harm.

There are multiple entry points to this topic, and making the decision about where to start begins with assessing how much your students already know about the topics presented in the text. If your students do not have much exposure to the topic of police brutality, it might be a good starting point to begin there rather than an immediate shift to spirit-murdering. What follows are a series of ideas and activities that teachers can use to delve deeply into *All American Boys* and the concepts of death and spirit-murder in young adult literature.

These ideas are by no means an exhaustive list and they are designed to help educators find a way into the text at the pace and climate that works best for students. Educators should treat these ideas as flexible and still part of a larger effort to create an anti-racist classroom space.

Meeting Students Where They Are

In pursuit of the goals of having an anti-racist space that challenges how teachers think about and teach about death, this series of tasks begins with a reflective prewriting activity that asks students to consider their observations and experiences with race and racism.

These prewriting prompts should be curated by teachers for their classrooms, but there are teaching resources available to assist teachers with framing their initial thoughts. Educator and writer Jon Greenberg's (2017) website for Citizenship and Social Justice (http://citizenshipandsocialjustice.com/) has an extensive reading list and sample curriculums that can help teachers to begin crafting lessons related to the impact of racism.

It is important that teachers participate fully in these tasks, from planning to participation, because it acknowledges their own participation and disruption of the system of racism, which helps to contribute to an anti-racist curriculum. When teachers and students share responses, it is important to note that some students may not feel comfortable with doing so, especially if they are one of few students of color in the classroom space.

It is essential that teachers emphasize that the purpose of sharing these narratives is not to debate whether racism still exists, but rather to acknowledge the presence of a system that has constraints and affordances for different groups of people. Students of color feel ostracized in discussions about race because there is an undertone of disbelief about the existence and stress of racism. Yet, the aim here is to start from a different space, which could possibly help students feel comfort in sharing.

After sharing the initial responses, teachers can push the dialogue further by discussing the prevalence of racism in both public and private spaces. Teachers can ask questions such as: How does racism show up when applying for a job? Driving a vehicle? Or buying a car? An anti-racist teaching framework takes into consideration the apparent sensitivity of sharing stories of racialized trauma from the perspective for both those who it is intended to harm and those who benefit from its presence. Teachers should strongly advocate and prioritize student agency in that students are not obligated to share every moment publicly, but there are moments where their work will have an audience. An opt-out option for this unit, whether it be in terms of writing about spirit-murder and sharing their thoughts about *All American Boys*, does not support the mission of an anti-racist framework. Choosing to not address racism, spirit-death, because of student or teacher discomfort, is how the structure of racism stays afloat.

An anti-racist classroom demands that teachers and students study how acts of racism include more than individual actions. Specifically, how is racism embedded in daily, normalized interactions? Brave New Films, a nonprofit organization that produces educational films, has a YouTube film called *Racism Is Real* that unpacks these questions using data from how racism affects its victims in terms of access and economic security. Teachers can use this resource as a way of interrogating the multiple ways that people encounter racism.

From there, teachers can ask students to consider what would be the emotional impact of racism upon a person? Either through a writing assignment or discussion, it should be stressed that the emotional impact of racism goes further than being uncomfortable and annoying. Asking students to think about the emotional toll of racism will be profound in their subsequent reading of *All American Boys*.

During Reading: Reading *All American Boys*

In conjunction with our objectives around critical reading strategies, it is imperative that we pause at certain parts of the book that detail the impact of spirit-murder. At this point, student should receive a working definition of spirit-murder and some of physical and emotional symptoms that accompany these actions. As they are reading from Rashad's account, they can use a double-entry journal to mark the instances of symptoms listed earlier in the chapter. As students read the chapters, they will reflect upon and record the short- and long-term effects police brutality toward Rashad and how it can be connected to current cases of police brutality.

For example, in table 4.1 are three incidents that would be a good place for teachers to pause and consider how these sections could inspire a refined conversation around death.

Equally as critical to this exploration of race-based violence is understanding Quinn's role in the text. It is necessary in an anti-racism classroom to pick apart not only how the victim is affected by the physical and mental strain of racism but also how the silence of our friends contributes to the system of racism. Along with marking Rashad's temperament, teachers should encourage students to think about Quinn's struggle in terms of witnessing the beating and subsequently telling the truth. Teachers should consider pairing this annotation of the text with the historical narratives of individuals who were also witnesses to the impact of police brutality.

For example, teachers could create teachable moments around stories like Rodney King and Eric Garner, both of whom were beaten or killed by the police on camera. The untold stories of the men who were filming these atrocities can be attached to Quinn's story by asking the following questions:

- What if Rashad's beating had not been witnessed by Quinn? How would this story have shifted?
- What is the connection between spirit-murder and silence? What is the role of silence in the continuation of systemic racism?

Table 4.1. Three Examples of Spirit-Murder and Racism to Consider

Quote from All American Boys	Connection to Spirit-Murder and Racism
"Yeah he was trying to steal those chips!" the clerk interrupted. "Isn't that right? Isn't that what you were trying to do? Isn't that what you put in your bag?" (p. 21).	The gas station clerk assumed that a black male in the store equates to theft. The consistent assumption of theft against people of color is a form of spirit-murder.
"My brain exploded into a million thoughts and only thought at a time— please don't kill me" (p. 23).	The trauma of police brutality extends beyond physical beating for Rashad. There is often a silent and unacknowledged fear of the loss of life when people of color encounter the police. What will Rashad expect the next time a police officer approaches?
"Everybody was asking that, as if I was ever going to tell them the truth. Nobody wanted to hear the truth, even though everybody already knew what it was. I felt . . . violated."	Having to defend yourself in a situation that caused by racial profiling and not being able to tell anyone how it feels is a pervasive form of trauma that can have physical and psychological harm.

Postreading *All American Boys*

The ideas mentioned previously on how to bring up spirit-murder in *All American Boys* can transition into an analysis of other characters in literature. In box 4.1, there are other novels mentioned that could be used to teach this concept. The impact of bringing spirit-murder into a classroom discussion is that teachers are complicating the ways in which death is discussed, including the idea that emotional and spiritual deaths exist.

CAUTIONS AND ADVICE

Teachers are risk-takers. As such, that risk-taking comes with some massive cautionary moves around the curricular decisions that one makes whether it is text-selection or the ways students express their thoughts. Talking and teaching about race can be difficult. However, the risk of not doing so will guarantee racism's viability.

Teachers should be forewarned that embarking on a discussion of spirit-murder and the impact of racism is task that is couched with purpose and vulnerability. Interest in this topic has to be sustained beyond having something "different" to teach. What makes this chapter different from the others in this book is that readers may all have some experience with death, but not all have experienced the impact of racism from the perspective of spirit-murder. Knowing this, initiating this quest means that teachers have to embark on a quest to learn about their role in systematic racism—either as victims or silent participants.

Vulnerability is a requirement for selecting this work as part of your curriculum. This lesson on spirit-murder seeks to dismantle the silence around racialized acts of violence by asking both teachers and students to theorize about their experiences, and at times, their complicity. This work demands that all become both teachers and learners, in order to move toward a more nuanced, intersectional framing of death.

CONCLUSION

An act of racialized police brutality is spirit-murder, a form of recurring emotional death. And this form of death is not something that teachers should bypass in literature but rather take up with a sense of urgency because of its closeness to the world students (and teachers) live within.

There are numerous back-to-back examples of spirit-murder in society and in literature, and teachers should take the risk of approaching this topic in their work with students. A discussion about police brutality and systemic racism can be a starting place to create a classroom, and eventually, a world that seeks justice. Additionally, changing how teachers ask students to write and annotate texts could help in recognizing how embedded this work is in our daily lives.

Therefore, an invitation is offered here. Teachers need to be brave in accepting this invitation to use the current political context and young adult literature to have open and frank conversations about death, in all of its variations. This will help educate our students about the complexities of race, racism, and spirit-murder.

BOX 4.1   CONNECTED RESOURCES

The Movement for Black Lives. (n.d.). The movement for black lives. Retrieved from https://policy.m4bl.org/

> This website, organized by the Movement for Black Lives, has an extensive list of policy demands and suggestions for how to interrupt and dismantle racism.

@samswey, @deray, & @MsPackyetti. (2017). Mapping police violence. Retrieved from https://mappingpoliceviolence.org/

> This site tracks instances of police violence against citizens in the United States and would be a helpful resource for students to analyze and understand data related to police brutality.

Brave New Films. (2015, April 29). *Racism is real* [Video file]. Retrieved from https://www.youtube.com/watch?v=fTcSVQJ2h8g&feature=youtu.be

> This informational video produced for young people is meant to give an overview of topics related to *All American Boys* and the concept of spirit-murder.

Ellison, R. (1965). *Invisible man*. London, UK: Penguin Books.
Magoon, K. (2014). *How it went down* (1st ed.). New York: Henry Holt and Company.
Morrison, T. (2004). *Beloved*. New York, NY: Vintage International.
Myers, W. D. (1999). *Monster*. New York, NY: Harper Collins Children's Books.

> These four above texts offer narratives that discuss the emotional and physical ramifications of racism and can be used to discuss how spirit-murder appears in literature.

REFERENCES

Galliers, D. (1987). A framework for anti-racist training. *British Journal of In-Service Education, 13*(2), 67–75.

Greenberg, J. (2017). Citizenship & social justice. Retrieved from http://citizenshipandsocialjustice.com/

Love, B. L. (2014). "I see Trayvon Martin": What teachers can learn from the tragic death of a young black male. *Urban Review, 46*(2), 292–306.

Pearce, M., & Thomas, D. (2015, October 27). Deputy who threw South Carolina student in class is under federal investigation. *The Los Angeles Times*. Retrieved from http://www.latimes.com/nation/la-na-girl-thrown-police-south-carolina-20151027-story.html

Reynolds, J., & Kiely, B. (2015). *All American boys*. New York, NY: Simon & Schuster.

Williams, M., & Leins, C. (2016). Race-cased trauma: The challenge and promise of MDMA-assisted psychotherapy. *MAPS Bulletin, 26*(1), 32–37.

Williams, P. J. (1991). *The alchemy of race and rights*. Cambridge, MA: Harvard University Press.

Winn, M.T. (2016, February 9). *Transformative justice: Transforming teacher education*. Paper presented at Teaching Works, Ann Arbor, MI.

Chapter 5

The Hate U Give: Experiencing Death and Grief in the Face of Social Justice

Tiye Naeemah Cort

Death and grief are usually not the first terms that come to mind when you think of your favorite book, but *The Hate U Give*, by Angie Thomas, examines the perspectives of death and grief through characters' struggles through loss and social justice challenges. Starr, the novel's female teen protagonist, is a character to whom students in high school classrooms can relate at every level. Dealing with the death of not only one, but two of her childhood friends, she goes through what many people experience once they encounter the death of a loved one personally or vicariously.

In the classroom, discussions of death and grief may cause feelings of vulnerability and discomfort because it is challenging to think through our understanding of death and the after effects of losing someone. Starr shows the expected signs of loss and grief through mixed desires to be alone and to seek comfort from others (Adler & Clark, 1991), yet her urge to hide feelings usually appears when she desires to appear strong and unaffected (Deminco, 1995).

This chapter includes instructional plans for use pre, during, and post reading *The Hate U Give*. Each section contains possible assignments, activities, and projects, focusing on the crucial emotions surrounding death and grief from violence as portrayed in the text. Educators can follow the guide while allowing space for appropriate supplemental materials for their specific groups of students. This chapter establishes following three goals to guide both educators and students:

- Developing a further understanding of the effects that death has on everyone, including those who are indirectly involved.
- Embracing agency in speaking and writing so students openly express feelings and reactions to death, grief, and the issues of both in the text.
- Connecting the book's events and those happening in the world today through critical reflection, discussion, and analysis.

SUMMARY OF *THE HATE U GIVE*

In the novel, *The Hate U Give* (Thomas, 2017), the author focuses on dealing with death from the perspective of the young adult main character, Starr Carter. Starr is already dealing with the death of a close friend, Natasha, a loss from which she assumes that she has already recovered. During a party, she reconnects with Khalil, an estranged childhood friend. During their drive home, they are pulled over by the police, and Khalil is subsequently murdered by the officer in a scene that is all too familiar in urban black communities.

As a witness to the murder, Starr deals with conflicting feelings about her involvement and reactions to Khalil's death. She learns through her own grief and the reactions of those around her—family, community members, and friends. The subsequent events of protests and demands for peace from both inside and outside of her community are consequences of death that address issues of social justice. Starr develops a newfound outlook on the world, all while navigating her duality as a girl living in a dangerous urban neighborhood and a minority student at a predominantly white suburban private school.

The multilayered experience of grief causes Starr to rethink her relationships, perspective, and identity in ways to which many people, especially adolescents, can relate. As she navigates her relationships with her boyfriend and family members, rethinks how much her friends understand and support her (especially those at school), and grapples with ideas of self-guilt in Khalil's murder and her duty to speak up in his defense, Starr undertakes important decisions that impact not only her life but also the lives of those around her.

Understanding the factors and perspectives that impact reactions to death will connect Starr's story to today's world and students' personal lives for the purpose of reflection through relating to the text.

TEACHING THE TEXT THROUGH A CRITICAL EYE

The Hate U Give is a novel that has excellent learning points that include societal factors and their influences on life and prejudice against black urban populations, living life between two very different communities, and the complexity of relationships. Throughout the story, Starr is constantly deciding what to say and what not to say in front of her friends from her community and those at school, sometimes out of fear that they will judge her negatively, making her feel alienated.

Starr lives what many may consider to be a dangerous life. She lives in an urban neighborhood where gang violence is commonplace. Her father,

Maverick, is a reformed gang leader who becomes involved in the rescue of young boys who refuse to remain involved in the community's warring gangs. This makes Starr a well-known person, which is something that works in her favor when it comes to protection but often gets in the way of her desire to have her own identity as more than "Maverick's daughter."

Starr's reputation at school is very different as one of few black students at her suburban high school. At school, she is quiet and cool, dating a wealthy white classmate, Nick, and her life outside the bubble of high school is relatively unknown. Her classmates know that she lives in the hood, but fail to acknowledge it until news breaks about Khalil's murder. The relationship that Starr has with her boyfriend, which is rooted in a love for 1990s' sitcoms, urban black film, and pop culture, turns into a deeper bond as they face the mixed reactions they receive as an interracial couple, including a negative reaction from her own father.

The family bond between Starr, her parents, siblings, and community members also deepens as everyone is touched and deeply affected by Khalil's murder and the legal, social justice, and personal consequences of such a tragedy emerge. The suggested activities focus on death and grief as presented in the novel. Students will explore how death affects Starr and all of those around her regardless of their proximity or their ability to connect with Starr.

Everyone either has or will encounter death and grieving at some point in their life. People deal with these difficult times in different ways. Students will look at different ways to think about and respond to death that pushes them to consider not only different perspectives but also the various circumstances that may influence how distinctly individuals respond to both death and grieving.

In *The Hate U Give*, Starr expresses her grief very differently at home from the way she expresses herself at school. When she is around her friends and family in her home community, she maintains her composure because she does not want to look weak. Death and violence are not uncommon at home, and she is accustomed to hearing about young black boys being killed as a result of gang violence. She is also accustomed to seeing people around her constantly in a state of grief that callouses them with a mask of strength to hide vulnerability.

She sees this in her half-brother's sister, Kenya, who lives with her mother and her abusive ganglord boyfriend. Kenya believes that such a living situation is "normal." Starr is accustomed to her proximity to violence and hearing it justified as "normal." Although Starr knows better, her exposure to this world and way of thinking impacts her need to be tough. Khalil's murder is not as much of a surprise as the effects of the posthumous widespread criminalization of her friend when allegations that he had a gun are presented as evidence to justify his killing.

At school, Starr attempts to maintain her composure. She knows that her classmates don't understand her community, why she does not initially publicly acknowledge her identity as "the witness," and why she does not support their use of Khalil's murder as a reason to stage superficial protests that are not rooted in the same truth as the real protests happening back home.

Thus, Starr remains silent about her relationship with Khalil and her involvement as a witness since she knows that her friends who are so removed from her community will not identify with her need to code switch, her "snitches get stitches" mind-set, or her need to separate her home life from her school life.

Contemporary media shows scenes of death and grief, but in reality, life does not go back to normal after one scene. We grow from both positive and negative experiences, and we change as a result. For this reason, each of the activities presented in this chapter is to be completed over the course of multiple class periods. This allows time for students to prepare for reflection and thought to make bigger text-to-world connections. This structure also allows time for teachers to evaluate and periodically assess student learning and understanding of death, grief, and the bigger picture social justice issues of race, class, and representation.

This chapter will guide both educators and students in the following:

- Developing a further understanding of the effects that death has on everyone, including those who are indirectly involved.
- Embracing agency in speaking, writing, and freely and openly expressing feelings and reactions to death, grief, and the issues of both in the text.
- Connecting, critically reflecting, discussing, and analyzing both the book's events and those happening in the world today.

Before diving into discussions of death, space will be allowed for reflection on personal experiences through writing prompts that will help guide students in exploring emotions, thoughts, and reactions to death using information from the text as well as current news sources. These writing prompts are included in the prejournal section.

Through these reflective writing activities, students will be prepared to the following:

- Consider how information received from different perspectives and sources may influence the perception of tragedy and the circumstances surrounding it.
- Transition into thinking, sharing, and relating to one another about their own direct personal experiences with death and grief through small group discussions and activities that guide in helping students identify similar reactions, emotions, and thoughts around loss.

- Identify and note questions that arise for consideration throughout the reading of the book. These same questions will be addressed as students discuss and further develop their thoughts and ideas around death and grief.
- Develop a main thematic question about death or grief, which they will keep in mind throughout the reading of the book, to be answered in the final activity.

The planned duration of these activities, which can be spread across the mentor text as well as any other supplemental materials, is meant to be two to three weeks (see table 5.1). This schedule factors in time allotted for students to read in class and have meaningful discussions during the different activities described.

Prereading: The Personal Reflection Journal

Whether students realize it or not, they have all been touched by the death of someone. Maybe it was someone as close as a friend or relative or someone more removed like a celebrity or a musician whose music they love. Even if there is no personal feeling of connection, every student, regardless of age, has dealt with death on some level even if only vicariously.

This journal allows students to think openly through their own experience with death and how it is/has been dealt with in their own lives. This will prompt students to think more about how death affects those close to the deceased and

Table 5.1.   Unit Plan Guide

Section	Activities		
Prejournal	Writing Prompt 1 (One day)	Writing Prompt 2 (One day)	
Prereading Activity	Social Media as a News Source (One day)		
Reading Activities	Character Relationship Chart (One to two days)	Relationship/ Reaction Discussions (One to two days)	
Main Activities	Did Khalil Have to Die: Justifying Death When Not Every Question Has an Answer (One to two days)	What If It Was My Friend: How Factors Change Stories (One to two days)	Moving on versus Forgetting: Finding Closure after Tragedy (One to two days)
Final Activity	Final Presentations (One week)		

everyone else around them. Further there are some guiding questions for students to consider while sharing their thoughts and experiences with death.

Teacher Discussion Points for Writing Prompt #1

People always try to imagine their reactions to different events before they happen. When someone dies, although people usually expect to be sad, upset, or desire to be alone for a while, lots of different emotions and feelings can emerge, sometimes unexpectedly. Whether writing about someone close to you or about someone whom you did not know personally, like a celebrity or other well-known person, think about the different people around them like their close friends and families and how they may react to death of someone close to them.

WRITING PROMPT #1

Think of the last time that you found out that someone died. It can be a loved one, someone you knew personally, or a complete stranger that you heard about in the news or on social media. How do you feel now thinking about that person and their death? Are those feelings and emotions what you expected after the death of a person? Name those feelings, emotions, and reactions, and explain why those may be initial responses to death.

Following this prompt, students should be allowed opportunities to share what they wrote. Suggesting that they share something that was surprising or something that they think that other students may be able to relate to is a great way to get some conversation going about personal reactions and feelings about death. This initial journaling and dialogue experience is something that they can continue to keep in mind while reading *The Hate U Give* as they encounter different characters' reactions and responses to death throughout their reading.

Since students are thinking about reactions to death on a personal level, the second writing prompt will begin a dialogue to connect them with reactions to death on a social justice level.

Teacher Discussion Points for Writing Prompt #2

Since the story focuses on the death of a young African American male, students will be better prepared to understand Starr's references to stories of black males dying at the hands of police if they conduct a bit of research about her references. Social media and the Internet are common news sources that often provide links to articles about different incidents and the reactions surrounding the deaths that took place as a result (e.g., Amadou Diallo, Manuel Loggins, Jr., Ronald Madison, Sean Bell, Eric Garner, Michael Brown, Jr., Alton Sterling, Philando Castile, Walter Scott, and Tamir Rice).

WRITING PROMPT #2

Using the Internet, students will find a news article about the killing of a young African American man in the United States at the hands of the police from the past ten years (it may also be helpful to have a few news articles on hand). Have students split into groups to read the articles together, and then discuss the following questions:

- What questions do you have around the circumstances of the story as it is being reported?
- What details seem unlikely or uncertain?
- Whose voice(s) is/are being heard in this piece?
- What social justice reactions took place following the death of this person?

After reading the article, consider three different perspectives on this same news story: that of a close family member, a childhood friend, and someone from outside of his community. How may the story be a bit different from each perspective?

Following this writing prompt, conduct a whole-class discussion about what students noticed, questioned, and critiqued about the articles. The point of this exercise is to help students realize that not only are these stories common, but also it begins to get students thinking about the different ways stories are told. The manner of the telling impacts perspective and how readers interpret news based on their relationship or situational perspective—as parent, a friend, a community member, and so on.

This journaling experience will be raw and vulnerable. Students know what they are expected to write and say, but teachers should push students to share beyond those surface feelings and responses. This may be easier for some students than others, but this is a great time for a writing conference. One-on-one brief conferences with students as they write allow for short, private moments with the teacher for students to share some of their thinking as they write it down.

The point during these conferences is not only to have students practice verbalizing their thinking but also to encourage students to expound upon the ideas and what they have written. More than asking follow-up questions, ask open-ended and subjective questions that build upon what students have already shared and how it connects to their experience.

Social Media as a News Source Activity

Everyone has the right to grieve when they experience loss. Whether you know the victim personally or not, people form their own personal connections that have lasting effects. People are able to share their feelings, thoughts, and opinions on any matter with a larger audience faster than before through access to social media and other digital platforms.

In *The Hate U Give*, Starr witnessed her friend's murder firsthand, and it was not the first time that she watched a friend die. She heard different accounts of what happened to Khalil through her friends' conversations at school even though she knew the truth. Starr quickly realized that the messages that news outlets sent and the truth that she knew were far apart.

News travels so quickly that stories are constantly in development even as they are being shared. This quick form of communication makes it possible for any and every one to have their say in the way a story develops. Keep this in mind as the class discusses grieving, who does it, and how it affects everyone around us. Using either the same or different person from the second writing prompt, students will explore reactions to the death of a black male through the use of Internet and social media resources. Students will search for the following:

- One online news story from a reputable news source.
- Social media reactions to the death on Twitter (hashtag searches will probably be most useful, e.g., #TamirRice).

In small groups, students can discuss their findings and the similarities and differences between the official news stories and reactions from everyday people. Students will share their findings and discussions with the class while taking note of the different ways that the stories are told and how people express their feelings about the incidents. What questions are being asked? What information is revealed? What speculations are being made? Encourage students to be critical in their thinking—asking why things are being said and making connections between both the news and social media sources.

Postreading Activities

Character Relationship Chart

The most obvious relationship chart to illustrate would be that of the different characters in relation to Khalil. Allowing students to determine their own way of representing the degrees of separation between characters in the book and Khalil will allow them to visualize how closely related every character is to the victim.

As students begin reading the story, instruct students to make a list of the characters who are named in the book leading up to Khalil's death. As the characters make their relationships with Khalil and the other characters around him known, ensure that students add these characters to their charts with some symbol to represent their proximity (family member, friend, etc.). For characters with no connection to Khalil or any other characters, students can list them outside of their chart.

Relationship/Reaction Discussions

As students add to their character relationship chart, they should consider the characters and their proximity to each other (e.g., Starr's friends at school versus Starr's proximity to the victim and the incident). Students will examine the situation from the main character's point of view, and they will eventually understand how death/tragedy has a domino effect on reactions (how the factors that impact grief and reactions of all of the characters are perceived throughout the story and the unexpected emotional responses characters have to Khalil's death, e.g., Starr's guilt about proximity to Khalil).

They will be able to identify critical points behind death to further develop their questions and analysis of Khalil's death.

Small Group Discussion

Now that students have created some visual reminder of how everyone is related, students will discuss the different ways that the characters that they have listed are dealing with Khalil's death. Although students do not have to write down their answers, they should take notes on what they are discussing with their groups and be prepared to share out their answers with the class during a subsequent whole-class discussion. Some questions to consider are as given here:

- What are the immediate reactions of those closest to Khalil?
- What are the immediate reactions of those who are not as close to Khalil (e.g., people outside of Khalil's community)?
- There is a difference in the responses to and justification of Khalil's death. What are the different responses and justifications of different characters, and how is this related to the characters' different relationships with Khalil?

Whole-Class Discussion

Students will share out what they discussed in their small groups, and this should turn into a larger discussion of the different ways that characters reacted to the death and connect the idea of reactions and responses to being

Table 5.2. Question to Consider

Character Reactions from Outside of the Community

Political backlash	There was a political backlash in response to the handling of Khalil's case that involved protesting. How does this relate to some of the grieving that was happening in Khalil's community?
Grieving from outside	For characters that are not directly related to Khalil, for example, the students at Starr's school, how are they affected by the grief of other characters? Are they allowed to grieve? If so, what makes it appropriate for them to respond to his death? What about for unnamed characters in the story, for example, police officers, school teachers, and administrators?
Misguided ideas of social justice	Starr felt a bit weird about the way her classmates responded to Khalil's death for many different reasons. Think of the reasons why she thought that their responses were inappropriate or misguided and discuss ways that her classmates could have responded more appropriately.

a part of grieving. The discussion of proximity and relationship should also be encouraged. Questions to consider adding to the conversation to get students thinking more outside of the box are included in table 5.2.

Encourage students to also think about characters who go unnamed (police officers, teachers, school administrators, etc.)

DID KHALIL HAVE TO DIE? JUSTIFYING DEATH WHEN NOT EVERY QUESTION HAS AN ANSWER

Although *The Hate U Give* is a fictional book, it is relatable to many students since it is reflective of events that many of us—people of color who live in or have personal connections to others in urban communities—unfortunately, often encounter. To further prove this point, a nonfiction text like *Between the World and Me* is a great supplemental text to have students read and explore. Drawing connections between the fiction and nonfiction texts is a great way to build upon the previous journalistic pieces that students read during the prejournal portion of their reading.

This activity will guide students in discussing questions that arise and evidence that shows which questions can and cannot be answered after a tragedy takes place. Students will continue to work on developing and answering questions about the killing and consider the effect that different justifications may have on grief and reactions of different characters and communities represented in the book, while drawing parallels between both texts and the real world.

Students will read an excerpt from *Between the World and Me* (Coates, 2015), where the author describes the killing of a former classmate and his own reactions to the unjustified death (pp. 75–85). This part of the text highlights some of the underlying major problems that are related to the loss of black male lives and connects to the case of Khalil's death. Coates describes the reputation of police presence in urban black communities and some of the thinking behind those impressions, which connects to other scenes in *THUG* (i.e., when two police officers approach Maverick and he is pinned to the ground and treated like a criminal in front of his children).

Main Activity

Students will read the piece individually, annotating and taking notes where necessary to highlight any points that they think may be important to further discuss or contextualize. If students do not own personal copies of the book, it may also be powerful to read these pages aloud to the class, having the students take notes while listening to the words being read.

Students will then split up into partners or small groups, where they will discuss different things that are described in the reading in light of past class discussions around death and grief:

• Similar to Starr, the author describes the loss of someone with whom he was no longer very close to yet somehow; Prince Jones' death touches him very deeply. In what ways does the author describe how the death of his former classmate deeply affects him?
• How has the death of Prince Jones changed or influenced Coates' mind-set about life and death?
• What are the similarities and differences between the ideas and thoughts that Coates describes and those of characters in *The Hate U Give?*

These discussions meet a variety of curriculum standards that involve drawing connections between texts, speaking critically about content and articulating thoughts about text in ways that will be useful beyond the classroom.

If not done beforehand, while students are engaged in their group discussions, teachers can post the two charts on opposite sides of the room. They should be titled as follows:

1. Similarities between Prince Jones' and Khalil's Deaths.
2. Differences between Prince Jones' and Khalil's Deaths.

Table 5.3.   Student Sample Responses

Similarities	*Differences*
Both are deaths at the hand of the police.	Prince Jones had no other witnesses besides the police officer. Starr witnessed Khalil's murder.
Both are remembered by loved ones as "good" people.	Prince Jones' killer claimed that he tried to run him over with his Jeep. Khalil's killer claimed that he thought he saw a gun in the car.
Both victims were driving and conducting completely innocent business (visiting a fiancée, dropping a friend home).	Prince Jones came from a "good" upbringing. Khalil was raised in what Starr called a "ghetto."
Both deaths prompted a move to activism (Prince Jones' mother said this at the funeral, Khalil's death prompted protests).	There is no information about whether Prince Jones' murder prompted backlash outside of his community. Khalil's death was used as an excuse for a walkout at Starr's suburban private school.

Students will circulate throughout the room adding their input to the lists. Students can feel free to write out words, complete ideas, draw pictures, or symbols to represent their ideas on each sheet. Following the completion of this activity, the class will reconvene and talk through the contributions that they have made to each chart. The teacher will point out some of the main points that students noted on the charts (maybe students circled or placed a check mark next to other students' words for emphasis), and encourage more discussion of the different elements from each story. Table 5.3 includes sample responses that students may add to the charts.

While the point is not to overdirect the students in filling in these charts, it is also important for them to compare and contrast this small excerpt from Coates' book with the reading that they have done so far. Once students have read to the point where they are reading reactions and statements from other characters that highlight race, class, and other societal factors, they should be prepared to contribute to these charts and participate in healthy dialogue about not only the killing of these men but also the other questionable circumstances surrounding their lives and deaths.

WHAT IF IT WAS MY FRIEND? HOW FACTORS CHANGE STORIES

Once students have self-reflected and explored the story and some nonfiction examples of similar events, the activities come full-circle to a more personalized perspective on death and grieving. Students can consider factors that are briefly mentioned in the text, such as race, socioeconomic status, neighborhoods, and access, and if/how they affected responses to Khalil's death. The point of this exercise is to get students thinking more from inside the stories that are being told than as innocent onlookers to tragic events.

Considering the victims of crimes as humans, and just as human as themselves, students may be able to make deeper connections to the stories being told. This will prompt critical thinking about the circumstances and aftereffects of death, tragedy, and grief. Using the text and other media resources, students will consider if Khalil was actually a friend of theirs who suffered the same plight. How would those same factors influence their response? The media's response? The responses of communities to which they belong?

Main Activity

To explore how societal factors impact the way stories are told, students will use online resources to find news about young people who were killed at the hands of the police. During their search, they should be looking for news articles about events that have happened over the past ten years. Once they have found at least five articles, some things that they should keep in mind are as listed here:

- What are the similarities between all of these articles?
- Do the victims have any commonalities? Are the circumstances similar?
- How familiar were you with the names of these victims before this assignment?
- What details are the journalists deciding to include in these pieces to make sure that readers receive the story in a certain way?

The class will discuss their findings, and this is something that can also be connected to the activity that identified the similarities and differences between Khalil's and Prince Jones' deaths.

MOVING ON VERSUS FORGETTING: FINDING CLOSURE AFTER TRAGEDY

Students will consider if and how it is possible to find closure in death situations that are common (prolonged illness, old age or, unfortunately police killings) that happen to involve someone close to us. For example, Starr never found any answers to what happened that night, but was Starr able to seek and ultimately find some kind of closure? What steps did she take in understanding what happened? How did other characters in the story find closure?

Final Activity

For the final activity, students will complete a final project and presentation that ties all of their work and discussions about the text together. Teachers can modify and further specify the different elements, but the project will include a reflective written piece about their growth in understandings of death and grief throughout the activities (connecting to the prejournal reflection writing) and one of the following options:

- A visual representation of the connections made between the student's life, *The Hate U Give*, and at least one of the nonfiction supplemental readings from class (news article, excerpt from *Between the World and Me*, etc.).
- A conceptualized piece (written, visual, or otherwise representative) that details the different ways of grieving as shown in examples throughout the text and how grieving people find closure.

Students will present their projects to the class, explaining their learning about death and grief throughout the reading of *The Hate U Give*.

CAUTIONS AND ADVICE

It is important to make sure that students feel safe and comfortable talking about their personal experiences with death and grieving and making sure that opportunities are always available for students to make connections throughout the reading of this novel. Death and grief are topics that cause feelings of vulnerability and discomfort, so allow space and time for students who need it. It may help to designate a space in the room for students to briefly remove themselves from the activities if necessary.

As the teacher, much of your role in the class dialogue is as a constant presence of encouragement and understanding, particularly when discussing difficult topics like death, grief, and social justice issues that arise in discussions. If students are shying away from discussing difficult topics of race, class, and prejudice, ask questions to challenge their thinking and encourage deeper responses. To get a sense of the connections that students are making, it will help to begin and end each class with an activity that allows students to reflect and share on what they are learning and connecting to their own lives.

Teachers should consider their rubrics and grading points while assessing student learning and understanding of the material. Since discussing feelings and emotions can sometimes be sensitive and personal material, students may be reluctant to share and participate, so some of the activities may be graded differently than others.

CONCLUSION

By the final activity, students will have analyzed the different aspects of grieving as they are expressed in the novel through reflection and discussion of the story and how a character's death impacts the story and the lives of everyone involved. By connecting this learning to nonfiction texts, students will be able to further bridge their classroom learning experience with that outside of school.

BOX 5.1   CONNECTED RESOURCES

Black lives matter. (n.d.). Retrieved from https://blacklivesmatter.com/

> The Black Lives Matter website is an excellent resource for information about a powerful movement that organizes people from different communities around the world to fight for social justice. This group fights for justice in cases similar to Khalil's in *The Hate U Give*.

Cort, T.N. (2014, December 18). In response to . . . [Blog post]. Retrieved from https://www.theblackeducator.com

> This blog post is one that was posted following the murder of Michael Brown, Eric Garner, and various other unjustified killings of black men whose cases ended without indictments against the police officers who killed them. It is written from the point of view of a black educator who had a candid discussion with her students.

Lane, T. Y., Chiarelli-Helminiak, C., Bohrman, C., & Lewis, T. (2017). The teachable moment: Engaging students in social justice movements. *Social Work Education, 36*(4), 359–72.

> This article discusses the work that social worker faculty did on one campus to get students involved in social justice work through the facilitation of dialogue both inside and outside of the classroom.

Johnson, C. (2014). The loss of friends to homicide and the implications for the identity development of urban African American teen girls. *Clinical Social Work Journal, 42*(1), 27–40.

> This article explores the identity development of urban black adolescent girls who have experienced the loss of a friend to homicide. Similar to the description of Starr's life following Khalil's murder, the study analyzes the different narratives of twenty-one girls and the ways that their experiences impact their identity development, coping mechanisms, and reactions to societal response to the homicide.

Mapping police violence. (n.d.) Retrieved from https://mappingpoliceviolence.org

> This website is a great resource for finding statistical information about the number of killings by police, locations, results of trials, and other important relevant information.

REFERENCES

Adler, E. S., & Clark, R. D. (1991). Adolescence: A literary passage. *Adolescence, 26*(104), 757–68.

Coates, T. (2015). *Between the world and me* (1st ed.). New York: Spiegel & Grau.

DeMinco, S. (1995). Young adult reactions to death in literature and life. *Adolescence, 30*(117), 179–85.

Thomas, A. (2017). *The hate u give.* New York, NY: HarperCollins Children's Books.

Chapter 6

A Murder That Sparked a Movement: Discussing Death in *Getting Away with Murder*

Jackie Mercer

On a hot Mississippi night in August 1955, fourteen-year-old Chicago native Emmett Till was kidnapped from his bed at his uncle Mose's house, never to be seen again. Till was brutally beaten and ultimately murdered by J. W. Milam and Roy Bryant for whistling at twenty-one-year-old Carolyn Bryant. Later that year on December 1, Rosa Parks refused to give up her seat on a Montgomery bus, which marked the start of the 381-day Montgomery bus boycott. Parks said about her decision to refuse to stand, "I thought about Emmett Till, and I could not go back."

Eight years to the day after Till's death on August 28, 1963, Martin Luther King, Jr. gave his famous "I Have a Dream" speech at the March on Washington, a not-so-subtle commemoration of Till's death, further solidifying his murder as the spark that ignited the civil rights movement.

In his book *Invisible Man*, Ralph Ellison (1952) begins, "I am an invisible man . . . I am invisible, understand, simply because people refuse to see me" (p. 3). Because of the color of his skin, Emmett Till's death, a death that has been acknowledged as the catalyst for the civil rights movement, was an all but forgotten piece of history.

Although his mother, Mamie Till Bradley, insisted on an open-casket funeral so that everyone would "see what they did to my boy," the highly publicized death of a black teenager took years to receive its due attention by the public. His murderers were the first white men to be put on trial for such a crime in the state of Mississippi, and despite the significance of this case, his death fell into obscurity for nearly fifty years before happenstance led to a new found interest in the case—including the publishing of two young adult books about his murder, *Mississippi Trial, 1955* and *Getting Away with Murder: The True Story of the Emmett Till Case.*

Emmett Till's story is not unique in many ways. Hundreds, if not thousands, of black men, women, and children were murdered across the American South simply for being black. Yet, Till's more public death shone a brighter light on the fact that in this country, some deaths carry more significance than others do. The life of a black or brown person historically has been construed as less significant in society than that of a white person, and as a result, the death of a black or brown person is also viewed by white society as a whole as less significant.

SUMMARY OF *GETTING AWAY WITH MURDER: THE TRUE STORY OF THE EMMETT TILL CASE*

In this literary nonfiction work, Chris Crowe (2003) tells the true account of the Emmett Till's murder. The original version published in 2003 was released before the FBI investigated the case from 2004 to 2006. A revised version of the book, which includes new information about the case from the FBI investigation, was released in early 2018 and provides a chronicle of the days leading up to the whistling incident, Till's kidnapping and murder, and the trial that followed.

This is not a simple retelling of a historical event. The author pulls his young adult audience into the narrative by humanizing Till, spending chapters describing parts of pop culture that would have been important to Till and talking about Till's interests.

True to the request of Emmet's mother, the book does not shy away from the more brutal aspects of the murder, incorporating several photos including the famous photo of Till's mutilated body in the casket. The readers are respected as young adults who are capable of handling death, and who deserve to know just how horrific and unjustified this murder was.

DEVELOPING SYMPATHY AND EMPATHY THROUGH CLOSE READING

Some students are not adequately taught about the civil rights movement, nor do they learn about the murder of Emmett Till. In his study of American history textbooks, Loewen (2007) found that in many cases, the events and key figures of the 1960s—including major civil rights leaders—"gets fewer than 35 pages" of the book (p. 214). Unfortunately, not much has changed as recent surveys of high school textbooks have found little, if any, space is given to Emmett Till's story, let alone others.

If students are not familiar with the history of instances of racism that have plagued our country and the movement to end discrimination in this country, it is impossible for them to begin to understand the significance of Emmett Till's death or any other story dealing with the unjustified murder of a person of color. Building students' background knowledge of the time period and pulling on their prior knowledge is a key component at the beginning of this unit.

Loewen (2007) argues that history is composed of "fantastic and important stories" (p. 2), but that students are bored in the classes that present these stories. Plus, the stories of Martin Luther King Jr. and Rosa Parks have been covered repeatedly throughout their academic lives, so it is fundamental to build interest in a forgotten, yet monumental, civil rights event.

Prereading: Exploring the Mississippi Delta

To fully understand Emmett Till's murder, its place as a primary catalyst for the civil rights movement, and the reasons for it being all but dropped from our nation's history for so long, students need to first understand what the Mississippi Delta and the South were like. It is also important for students to begin to consider how in 1955 a fourteen-year-old black boy from Chicago could arrive in a small Delta town—Money, Mississippi—and be murdered in less than a week.

Students meet several literacy standards throughout the course of a small research project (box 6.1) about the Mississippi Delta before they read about Emmett Till. Each student is assigned a particular topic dealing with the Mississippi Delta. They must research, report, and then teach their peers about their particular topic.

Kelly Gallagher (2009) notes that there is a difference between students' simply memorizing facts and knowing history and "teachers turning students into deep thinkers" (p. 10). So even though reading is a "primary way to know things" (Lemov, 2017, p. 10), being required to then teach others about that information is even more effective for the retention of information. Students are encouraged to become focused on retaining knowledge in order to teach it to others instead of simply completing an assignment to have it finished (Lemov, 2017, p. 16).

After completing some primary research about the area of the country in which Emmett Till was murdered, a close study of the life, death, and historical significance of Till is framed by four essential questions:

- Why are some deaths considered more tragic than others?
- Why should students still learn about Emmett Till sixty years after his death?
- How does death connect us as humans?
- How are prejudices and biases revealed through our reactions to death?

The purpose of the essential questions is to provide students with overarching ideas to explore throughout the course of the unit. A discussion about Emmett

Till's death is not simply about his death, but about the larger social issues that led to his death, the ways that these social issues still manifest themselves in our society today, and how our own experiences and prejudices may create a bias about the value of a person's death.

BOX 6.1   MISSISSIPPI DELTA MINI-RESEARCH PROJECT

Task: Select a topic from the following list. Research your person, place, event, and so on, and teach your classmates about that particular topic.

Process:

- After researching your topic, create a page on the class Google Site for your topic where you discuss what you found in your information.
- Be sure to have answered all applicable questions for your topic. Each category of topics has its own set of questions.
- Properly cite all material that came from research.
- Include a minimum of three pictures related to your topic. Include a caption under each.
- Be prepared to speak for five minutes about your topic. You are the teacher.

Topic Categories:

- Music of the Delta
- People of the Delta
- Culture of the Delta
- Events in the Delta
- Place in the Delta

During Reading

Once students have learned about the area of the country where Emmett Till's murder happened, students will begin discussing the essential question how do we define nonfiction and what is the difference between truth and fact. This discussion activates prior knowledge because students have encountered nonfiction before and have usually learned that nonfiction means that something is true.

Learning Historical Context

Before reading *Getting Away with Murder*, students watch a 1980s documentary from PBS, *Eyes on the Prize* (1987), which contains several instances of misinformation about the event, including a cousin who made false claims about what happened at the Bryant's grocery story the day Emmett Till whistled—but who actually was not even present when the events took place.

After viewing the documentary, the teacher asks students to consider the fact that many of the details presented are blatantly false (box 6.2). This challenges their preconceived notions about nonfiction and opens the door for conversations about several topics, including the validity of sources and the need to check several sources for inconsistencies before coming to a conclusion about a topic.

BOX 6.2   COMMON MISTRUTHS ABOUT EMMETT TILL AND HIS MURDER

- Curtis Jones, a cousin of Emmett Till, was present at Bryant's Grocery at the night of the whistling incident.
- Emmett Till asked Carolyn Bryant for a date and said other inappropriate things to her.
- Mose Wright identified Roy Bryant and J. W. Milam in court by pointing and saying, "Thar He."

Developing Close-Reading Skills

The reading and consuming of nonfiction sources is more difficult than fiction in a myriad of ways. Students do not tend to have as much exposure to nonfiction text as they do to fiction in their academic careers. Nonfiction texts ask students to consider what biases or pieces of misinformation they might be presented in the text (Beers & Probst, 2016, p. 19). By no fault of their own, students may not have the familiarity with nonfiction texts to even understand how to begin analyzing the reading.

It also is sometimes difficult for students to analyze nonfiction because they are generally not presented with nonfiction in a way that asks them to critically analyze the writing. Students may appear to be resistant to the types of intellectual work, which lead to a deeper understanding of a text because they are overwhelmed by the task in front of them, because they have never been taught the skills necessary, or both.

The essential questions for the unit demand a deeper understanding of complex topics, so while reading the text, the teacher must walk students through this process. For each chapter of the book, students are provided with a question sheet that walks them through a basic, surface-level understanding of the text along with a few questions, which lead students into deeper thinking. Students have the chance to answer these guided reading questions and discuss them; however, students are asked to grapple with the difficult task of close reading and analysis on their own before bringing their work back to discuss with the entire group.

Beers and Probst (2016) outline several nonfiction signposts or markers "that alert [readers] to some significant moments in most nonfiction, those moments in which we need to think critically about claims an author makes" (p. 116). These signposts are Contrast and Contradictions, Extreme or Absolute Language, Numbers and Stats, Quoted Words, and Word Gaps (Beers & Probst, 2016, p. 116). Students are provided with a handout that defines each of the signposts and also gives them ideas of what questions they should be asking when they see an example of a signpost in a text.

For each chapter of *Getting Away with Murder*, students are asked to look for multiple signposts, consider why the author included that particular piece of information, and then consider the ways in which that signpost influences or affects a reader's understanding of a text. Students are also required to look for a variety of different signposts because some are more challenging than others; they are not allowed to constantly focus on the ones that are easier for them. Students have to have the chance to grapple with the text and complex ideas instead of simply just being told the answer (Beers & Probst, 2016, pp. 32–33).

Postreading

While reading the text, students spend time reflecting on the essential questions, but the bulk of grappling with those complex issues comes after the text is finished. After students have had a chance to work through the signposts and analyze the text using a chart, such as the example provided in table 6.1, the entire class discusses their findings. At the end of each chapter, students are asked to reflect upon and write about their thoughts about the essential questions as a result of the reading they have completed.

In addition to reading Crowe's (2003) book, students are also provided with excerpts from other books about the case such as Devery Anderson's (2015) *Emmett Till: The Murder That Shocked the World and Propelled the Civil Rights Movement* or Simeon Wright's (2010) *Simeon's Story*. These excerpts from historians and others who are providing firsthand accounts are contradictory in nature.

This leads the class to discussions about the validity of eyewitness testimony, the effect time has on the memories of witnesses, and the importance of the research completed by historians before their work is published. The

Table 6.1. Signpost Chart: Produced and Created by Jackie Mercer

Please do not use a signpost more than twice. Fill in each section as completely as possible. (Created by the author)

Nonfiction signpost	Example (with page number)
Analysis of signpost (answer to one or more of the questions for the Signpost) **WHY** is this significant? **HOW** does it influence our reading of the text and/or understanding of the event person, place, etc.	

Nonfiction signpost	Example (with page number)
Analysis of signpost (answer to one or more of the questions for the Signpost) **WHY** is this significant? **HOW** does it influence our reading of the text and/or understanding of the event person, place, and so on?	

goal is to broaden the students' understanding of what nonfiction is and to help them internalize the process of questioning source material and seeking out multiple sources on the same topic for comparison.

Because Emmett Till's death happened so long ago, it is easy for students to look at the event and recognize how horrific it was. After talking about Emmett Till, the conversation turns to more about the civil rights movement. Again, students can look at different cases of racially motivated crimes and agree those were wrong. The struggle comes in moving the conversation into the present day.

The last chapter of *Getting Away with Murder* focuses on the importance of the case in the twenty-first century. Students seem to struggle most with Till's story when modern-day examples are provided, such as Trayvon Martin and Tamir Rice. The students feel like they can connect to Till because he was close in age to them at his death and his story is history. The students do not seem to see Emmett Till as the "other" and they feel a sense of grief over his death. Many of them comment on how angry they are that justice never happened. They express sorrow for Mamie Till Bradley.

But the story is still distant for many of them, and they cannot connect with the perils of being black in America in the twenty-first century. The goal, of course, is that students will be able to see how they felt about issues from which they felt further removed, and then recognize similarities in situations that are happening today.

After reading the book and excerpts from other texts about Till, students are asked to consider what factors made the case so important to starting the movement. They are then asked to consider why such an important event was all but forgotten in history. This, of course, is where more difficult conversations about today's society come in. Although not all students are going to be able or willing to try to understand someone different from them, the goal is that the seed has been planted and someday they will be able to think about topics in different ways and gain some understanding of themselves and their unperceived biases.

CAUTIONS AND ADVICE

Racism has not been eliminated from American society. Studies suggest that "for the first time in this century, young white adults have less tolerant attitudes toward Black Americans than those over thirty" (Loewen, 2007, p. 163). Loewen (2007) suggests that one reason people are becoming more racist is because young people do not understand the history of the civil rights movement and how racism operates in our society today.

One result of this lack of knowledge and the resulting racism is that white people do not understand how to grapple with the death of a black person. Instead of grief over a death, they feel as if they are being shamed for their whiteness and are therefore left feeling angry and resentful.

Another suggestion is that people do not understand racism or are racist because it is implied throughout their education that the problems of the past such as slavery and discrimination no longer exists, so "race relations have somehow steadily improved" on their own as our society has evolved and are no longer an issue (Loewen, 2007, p. 163).

It is also possible that students are unaware of the "institutional white privileges benefitting white Americans that exist largely unnoticed" (Schieble, 2012, p. 212). Discussing Till's death and the casual nature of its treatment despite its role as a catalyst for the civil right movement is one way to highlight this for students. Looking at similar cases in the twenty-first century is a way to highlight issues that still exist.

Whatever the cause, the existence of racism as a part of the fabric of our society makes it uncomfortable to discuss the civil rights movement and modern-day examples of racially motivated murders. It is imperative for teachers to address controversial subjects and help students "realistically examine the complex issues of past and present racial discrimination" (Cipollone, 2006, p. 13); however, it is not always easy. After completing the unit about Emmett Till, the civil rights movement, and modern-day issues, students were surveyed about their beliefs about the unit and about racism in the country.

Many of the students expressed gratitude for the learning that took place and the modern-day connections they were able to discuss. Some, however, did not react as amicably. One commented that students felt as if the teacher was trying to "make us feel guilty for being white." Another commented that "Black lives matter is a joke. All lives matter." And one particularly alarming piece of anonymous feedback contained several racist comments while the student denied being racist:

> I believe that racism goes both ways and believe black people take advantage of their rights now and they should not be rioting. I believe we should bring the hoses back out and take them out. What racism back then and what it is now are totally different so you can not compare it. I believe you enforced the fact the all whites are racist, but that's not true because blacks are allowed in our schools and have rights so there is absolutely no reason for the black lives matter. I believe that it's terrible that people are thinking that but that not whites' fault. Just look at Youngstown [Ohio's] high crime rate and who lives there. Again I am in no means racist but I do believe that there is a big difference in a nigger and a black person and a black person who has a job and does not riot and demolish buildings and steal stuff. And there are just as many white niggers as there are black. I liked the Delta stuff but you really pounded the fact of racism and how it is today but I think you're wrong. They have rights but I do stand strongly against BLM, but thank you for the good year and do think you're a good teacher.

It can be defeating and disheartening to read comments like this after having spent so much time reading about and discussing the material. Despite the resistance from some students, no matter what is presented to them and how, "facilitating these critical conversations with young adult literature are key to helping students understand the concept of whiteness and racism in our country" (Schieble, 2012, p. 212). Framing the conversation is key. To alleviate potentially negative reactions from students, the teacher must address possible areas of concern ahead of time.

Even though students—particularly white students—may not realize it, many feel threatened or at a minimum uncomfortable when their place in society is put under the microscope. Students need to understand that being white is not inherently bad nor should they feel guilty, but they do need to understand it is the responsibility of everyone to recognize the institutions in our society that suppress other people.

Through the right books and through difficult discussions, students can "learn about their potential impact on society" (Cipollone, 2006, pp. 12–13), but they have to be able to see and understand how the themes in those books relate to their lives. They will be less willing, however, to do this; if they start the unit off thinking, it is meant to push the idea that all white people are racist.

Additionally, death of a young person is hard to discuss, but when race is part of the equation, it becomes even more difficult. When white students do not see the life of a person of color holding the same value as their own, they will struggle to see the death of a person of color as significant or as important as the death of a white person. Although as a society we would like to believe we have moved past these inherently racist attitudes, the murder of innocent black people, and the formation of groups like Black Lives Matter, it is clear we still have a long way to go.

CONCLUSION

Understanding our past is crucial to our ability to understanding ourselves, our society, and our world (Loewe, 2007, p. 2). Teachers have the moral obligation and social responsibility to bring to the forefront the complex and uncomfortable issue of racism and have open, informed conversations about it with students.

Emmett Till's story—his death—is still of monumental importance today. An examination of Till's case reminds us that if we can truly see each other as humans, regardless of skin color, then it is nearly impossible to dismiss the poor treatment—and in some cases, the cold-blooded murder—of people who we deem our equals. We owe that to our students and to our nation.

BOX 6.3   CONNECTED RESOURCES

Anderson, D. (2015). *Emmett Till: The murder that shocked the world and propelled the civil rights movement.* Jackson, MS: University Press of Mississippi.

A book twenty years in the making, it is considered the definitive work on the Emmett Till case. Although not a young adult book, selections from this nonfiction work can be used to supplement the information provided in Chris Crowe's texts.

Wright, S. (2010). *Simeon's story: An eyewitness account of the kidnapping of Emmett Till.* Chicago, IL: Lawrence Hill Books.

Firsthand account of the kidnapping of Emmett Till. Till's cousin Simeon Wright was in the bed with him the night J. W. Milam and Roy Bryant kidnapped him, and Wright tells the story not only of that night but also of the events leading up to and following the murder.

Crowe, C. (2002). *Mississippi trial, 1955.* New York, NY: Penguin Group.

A fictional account of Emmett Till's murder told from the perspective of sixteen-year-old Hiram Hillburn. Hiram begins to see the deep-seeded racism in the Delta he did not notice as a child and is torn between his deep love for and loyalty to his racist grandfather, and his inability to reconcile his grandfather's racism and his own beliefs.

REFERENCES

Ambrosino, M. (Producer), & Hampton, H. (Director). (1987). *Eyes on the prize: America's civil rights years 1954–1965* [Motion picture]. United States: PBS.

Anderson, D. (2015). *Emmett Till: The murder that shocked the world and propelled the civil rights movement.* Jackson, MS: University Press of Mississippi.

Beers, K., & Probst, R. (2016). *Reading nonfiction: Notice & note stances, signposts, and strategies.* Portsmouth, NH: Heinemann.

Cipollone, M. (2006). Creating engaged citizens: Using young adult novels and thematic units to encourage democratic action. *Afterschool Matters, (5),* 12–19.

Crowe, C. (2003). *Getting away with murder: The true story of the Emmett Till case.* New York, NY: Penguin Young Readers Group.

Ellison, R. (1952). *Invisible man.* New York, NY: Random House.

Gallagher, K. (2009). *Readicide: How schools are killing reading and what you can do about it.* New York, NY: Stenhouse Publishers.

Lemov, D. (2017). How knowledge powers reading. *Educational Leadership, 74*(5), 10–16.

Loewen, J. (2007). *Lies my teacher told me: Everything your American history textbook got wrong* (2nd ed.). New York, NY: Simon & Schuster.

Schieble, M. (2012). Critical conversations on whiteness with young adult literature. *Journal of Adolescent & Adult Literacy, 56*(3), 212–21.

Wright, S. (2010). *Simeon's story: An eyewitness account of the kidnapping of Emmett Till.* Chicago, IL: Lawrence Hill Books.

Part III

MASS TRAGEDIES

Chapter 7

Finding Closure through *Mockingbird:* When a Community Tragedy Is Personal

Lindsay Schneider

Grief is a highly personal and intimate affair; yet, often, this intimate moment also functions as shared experience and communal affair. Particularly when death strikes in mass (a school shooting, 9/11, or war), communal memorials and shared grief are often ubiquitous; yet, during this shared experience, there will always be those who are suffering a simultaneous personal grief.

How do teachers begin to navigate the waters with students when a national tragedy is personal tragedy? What can teachers do in the classroom in response to tragedies such as the 2018 Parkland shooting, 9/11, Katrina, and the Las Vegas shooting? How can teachers help students understand closure as it relates to the individual and the community?

By considering Kathryn Erskine's (2012) *Mockingbird*, secondary students will be given an opportunity to explore grief, hope, and closure as well as the specific societal concerns underlying school shootings through various lens and capacities. Furthermore, by reading and analyzing this text, students will grapple with its emotional impact and how grief and empathy can intersect in their own lives as well as within the community around them.

SUMMARY OF KATHRYN ERSKINE'S *MOCKINGBIRD*

Caitlin, a fifth grader with Asperger's syndrome, is doubly bereaved. Her mother passed away from cancer two years earlier; now her brother—her closest friend, confidant, and protector—has been fatally shot during a school shooting.

After overhearing a newscaster declare their community has found "closure" when a jury found enough evidence to put the boy who fatally shot

Caitlin's brother, Devon, during a school shooting on trial for murder, Caitlin is on a desperate search for closure of her own. Her search is further complicated as her father struggles to cope with his own grief and has difficulty navigating Caitlin's emotions and reactions.

Caitlin begins her search in vain; especially after her trusty dictionary fails to provide a clear definition for closure, she cannot grasp the elusive concept nonetheless experience it. Moreover, the social components of school become increasingly challenging without Devon's guidance, thus further hindering her ability to fully understand what is happening around her.

Caitlin's journey inadvertently takes a turn when her teacher encourages her to make new friends. Caitlin befriends a younger student, Michael, only to learn that his mother is the teacher who was also a victim of the same school shooting. Together, Michael and Caitlin begin to face the reality of their situations as well as learn to cope with the loss of their loved ones.

As Caitlin's quest continues, she is determined to finish Devon's Boy Scout project: an unfinished wooden chest. With help from her father and her teacher, Caitlin successfully completes Devon's project and is able to share it with the grieving school community. Through this process, Caitlin is finally able to define and create her own form of closure that is both personal and shared with others as she honors her beloved brother.

Students and teachers alike will be captivated by Erskine's (2012) honest prose. Embedded into this adolescent novel are themes that strike a chord with younger and older secondary students alike. As the book is told from Caitlin's first-person point of view, readers will begin to better understand how Asperger's syndrome can affect others as Caitlin works on social skills and makes friends. Readers will also be confronted with a deadly school shooting, loss of a family member due to cancer, bullying, and the power of empathy and hope.

TEACHING PERSONAL AND COMMUNAL TRAGEDY

Educating the head without educating the heart is no education at all.

—Aristotle

In order to teach through tragedies, teachers ought to discuss the ways in which books are both "head books" and "heart books" (Beers & Probst, 2017). In the classroom, teachers must value books not only for the ways in which they expand vocabulary and reading stamina or present the opportunity to grapple with a new idea or concept; rather they must also value and attend to books' ability to emote and forge a lasting impact on readers.

Educating the heart requires both attention and intention from both teachers and students.

Young adult literature (YAL) has a unique and valuable place in the secondary classroom; they are overwhelmingly relevant, timely, and captivating. YAL texts and stories connect with students on a personal level and often reflect the reality of their lives (Buehler, 2016). By using accessible and engaging texts, students are able to gain confidence and, therefore, dive deeper into rigorous analysis of the texts' themes and applications to the world around them.

Moreover, such an approach provides spaces for students to bring their own emotions and struggles into the classroom. YAL allows students to experience and empathize with others' tragedies as well as find comfort and coping strategies for their own. *Mockingbird* is no exception to this strategy. The text itself presents a quick read; yet, the topics of death, empathy, family, friendship, and grief encourage readers to slow down and truly consider the impact of this novel. *Mockingbird* moves beyond students' heads and into their hearts when they reflect on these themes.

While already relevant and apropos for teenagers' lives, YAL's insights and significance are forged when students read such texts in community. While reading alone, students immerse themselves in the text and connect to the characters and the world of the novel; while reading in community, students connect the text to their own lives and community while building deeper connections within their reading communities. Together, teachers and students create meaning beyond the pages of the texts; they build depth and significance that outlive a cursory reading of the text.

In reading communities, students and teachers alike have the opportunity to facilitate pertinent conversations about school shootings, mass tragedies and personal loss, and empathy while developing rigorous insights. Various strategies can be used to achieve this community including

- one-to-one student-teacher reading conferences,
- small-group literature circles,
- whole-class discussions, and
- partner reading journals in which students share a journal in which they write their own reflections on the text and respond to their partners.

The next section will consider prereading activities, textual analysis activities, and extension activities, which teachers can practically apply in the middle and high school classroom. The aim of these activities is to provide avenues through which teachers and students alike can explore the book itself, how the book impacts them intellectually, and how the book impacts their heart (Beers & Probst, 2017).

Prereading Activities

Research the Role of a Memorial as a Form of Closure

Just as Caitlin searches for closure, students can explore how nations or sub-cultures memorialize the dead in order to create closure. Students may begin by journaling about how they have memorialized those who have passed on in their own lives. Teachers may prompt students to consider the ways in which public services (e.g., a funeral) did or did not provide the student a sense of closure or peace. Likewise, students can reflect on how they personally remember a lost loved one: jewelry they wear, lighting candles, the effects of hearing a certain song, and so forth.

Following their personal reflection, students can expand their thinking to consider collective form of commemoration. Students can conduct research (see box 7.1) in groups or individually in order to present on the catalyst behind the memorial and how it affects the community. After presenting their findings, in small or large groups, students can discuss who is memorialized publicly once they have died and how closure can be a shared experience.

Students can further connect these ideas to personal accounts of the same deaths. For example, clips from the movie *Jackie* (2016) might be paired alongside the research of President Kennedy's funeral or worldwide news coverage of 9/11 might be considered alongside of family members of the deceased reflections of that day. By doing so, students can begin to understand the connections and differences between public and private mourning and grief.

Students can conclude with a writing activity on what they have learned about the role of memory as it connects to death, how community and

---

BOX 7.1   RESEARCH SUGGESTIONS

- Famous memorial services/funerals (e.g., Princess Diana, President John F. Kennedy, Rachel Joy Scott, and victims of the 1999 Columbine shooting)
- War monuments (e.g., The Franklin Delano Roosevelt Memorial, the 9/11 Memorial, and the National World War II Memorial)
- How various cultures memorialize the dead (ranging from the Egyptian pyramids to La Día de Los Muertes)
- Common headstones/epitaphs
- Social media hashtags, which memorialize someone who has died (#EricGarner, #TamirRice, #shawshooting, #16times)

individuals find closure, and how the two intersect. Students can choose to map out and even share their own journey of commemorating a lost loved one and their journey to closure.

Reading Strategies

The following activities consider methods teachers can use while students are reading the text. These suggestions encourage teachers and students alike to complete a rigorous analysis of the text while considering the themes of *Mockingbird* in ways that forge meaningful connections beyond the pages of the text.

The discussion topics recommended may take a variety of forms. Teachers may wish to have students independently journal their responses to the topics, work with one partner to discuss, facilitate small group discussions, create online blogs, which allow students to connect with students outside the school, conduct whole-class discussions, or hold one-to-one student-teacher conferences.

Discussion Topic: Aftermath of School Shootings

In pairs, students can identify passages in the text that speak to the aftermath of the school shooting. The teacher may then have students track and compare various characters' understandings of the shooting that takes place in the text and its aftermath. For example, using a fever chart, students might analyze Caitlin's process over time of understanding what caused Devon's death. Another option would be to have students create a chart to compare and contrast adult's responses such as Caitlin's father, Mrs. Brook, Michael's father, and the newscaster.

Discussion Topic: How an Individual Can Affect Their Community

Mockingbird can inspire students to work alongside others to seek out hope and create closure in the face of grief. Using *Mockingbird* as a springboard and mentor text can allow teachers the opportunity to guide conversations on empathy, interpersonal relationships, and the role of friendships and the interconnectedness between the three. Moreover, teachers can lead students in conversations that consider their day-to-day impact on those around them (see table 7.1).

Thematic Connections to To Kill a Mockingbird

By pairing *Mockingbird* with a classic text such as *To Kill a Mockingbird*, students will have the opportunity to truly explore the complexity of Kathryn

Table 7.1. Discussion Questions and Passages

Themes	Key Passage from Mockingbird	Discussion Questions
Empathy	"I'm mostly happy. . . . Even though I didn't think I'd like empathy it kind of creeps up on you and makes you feel all warm and glowy inside. I don't think I want to go back to life without empathy. . . . But I can't stop crying. For Devon. Because of what happened to Devon. Because his life got taken away and he can't do anything and he can't be happy or proud or live or love—and all of a sudden my gulp-crying turns into gulp-laughing because I realize something. . . . I'm not crying for ME! . . . I'm crying for Devon! I'm crying because I feel bad for HIM! Isn't that empathy? I'm feeling for HIM instead of me! . . . Empathy isn't as hard as it sounds because people have a lot of the same feelings. And it helps to understand other people because then you can actually care about them sometimes. And help them. And have a friend. . . . And do something for them and make them feel as good as you're feeling" (217–19). Other Passages: pp.123–28: "Empathy" (Entire chapter) p. 209: Josh crying on the playground p. 231: Michael, Josh, Mr. Schneider, and Mr. Smith playing football	At the end of the book, how does Caitlin define empathy? How do you define empathy? How can we develop empathy? How does empathy connect us to the people around us?
Interpersonal Skills	"Slowly Josh reaches his hand out and takes it from me. He even Looks At The Person this time. Thanks. You're welcome. Michael grins and whispers to me, Good remembering Your Manners. I nod. I don't even need the chart anymore. Not now that I know they're MY manners and I can do whatever I want with them" (223–24). Other Passages: pp. 136–43: Meeting Mr. Walters pp. 189–94: Group project in the computer lab	What is the significance of Caitlin learning how she is in control of her own manners? Throughout the text, Caitlin learns skills such as "Look at the Person," what is the importance of these skills? What are ways you can develop your own interpersonal skills in order to better connect with those around you?
Role of Friendship	"I don't really mind that Josh is sitting on the other side of Michael because even though he's not my favorite person he is nice to Michael. I take two gummy worms out of my pocket and give them to Michael. He smiles. This one's Caitlin and this one's Josh. When he says Josh's name I remember that Josh is Michael's friend. So I offer him a gummy worm too" (p. 223). Other Passages: pp. 170–79: "Friends" (Entire chapter) pp. 194–96: Michael's declaration that Caitlin is still his friend pp. 197–202: Michael's play	How does Caitlin's friendship with Michael affect her relationships with other people (specifically Josh)? What are small ways you can demonstrate or extend friendship? How does friendship affect Caitlin's fifth grade class both positively and negatively? How can your class build friendships that can include everyone? How can your friendship affect the community around you? How do friendships in the text lead to both individuals and the larger community finding closure following the school shooting?

Erskine's (2012) text. By finding points of connections between the text, students can facilitate a thoughtful discussion on why Erskine (2012) chose to allude to Harper Lee's (1960) text.

Students can explore and discuss the deaths of Mrs. Smith (Caitlin's mother) and Mrs. Finch compared to Devon and Tom Robinson by creating a Venn diagram leading to an analysis of the hatred that led to Tom's and Devon's death as opposed to death caused by illness. Students can also consider the roles of the deceased mothers and how the older brothers' (Jem and Devon) experience with their mother's death differs from their younger sisters' (Scout and Caitlin) who have few memories of/with their mothers. Some students may even choose to grapple with how role justice ought to manifest itself following Tom and Devon's deaths.

Extension Activities

Depending on the grade level and maturity of students, the following activities are intended to provide students with ways to consider the current climate surrounding school shootings and the ways in which teenagers can have an impact on both how a community finds closure surrounding such events and how teenagers can impact change in their own community as well as at the state or even federal level.

School Shootings Research

In her author's note, Kathryn Erskine (2012) explains how the Virginia Tech University shooting happened "in [her] own backyard" (p. 233). Unfortunately, this phenomenon is not uncommon: since 2013, there have been over 300 school shootings (Everytown for Gun Safety Support Fund, 2018). Particularly in a school setting, such an alarming statistic provides space for relevant research, evocative conversation, and substantial analysis.

From a research perspective, *Mockingbird* and Kathryn Erskine's commentary on the 2007 Virginia Tech shooting provide many avenues through which students can critically analyze data surrounding school shootings. The following activities encourage students to not only read and interpret data but to analyze what the data truly reveals. Teachers should approach such conversations with sensitivity and work alongside students as they grapple with the impact of the statistics.

To begin, students can research the number of school shootings as well as break down the data by level of school (elementary, middle, and high), number of fatalities and injuries, or any numbers of other factors. Depending on the age level and school community, teachers may also encourage students to consider the ways in which these data are represented (and perhaps manipulated) across a variety of news outlets. Particularly with older classes, students can create charts that compare and contrast their own district's or state's gun policies with others.

Students can further delve into the news articles surrounding school shootings and rhetorically analyze the subsequent media coverage as well as any long-term impacts on the school or community. Some examples may include the 2018 national student walkout, the school changing its name, opening of entirely new schools, or founding of clubs such as "Friends of Rachel"/ Rachel's Challenge.

Students might also analyze the rhetoric surrounding school shootings and its victims while also considering how such argumentation affects the loved ones of the victims, thus directly tying their research back to the text of *Mockingbird*. Consider whose voices are heard in the mainstream media and whose are excluded, how various political parties or figures respond to such tragedies, and how families/friends/classmates of the victims ensure their voices are heard.

A study of trending hashtags on social media following shootings such as #enoughisenough, #NeverAgain, #NationalSchoolWalkout, and #Enough may also provide compelling opportunities for students to reflect on the role of social media for raising awareness as well as provoking change. In light of recent shootings, students may also explore whether or not any laws (local, state, and federal) have changed as well as what teenagers specifically did to propel this change or the effect of social media on the national dialogue surrounding this issue.

Students can also create their own infographics to display either the prevalence or the impact of such tragedies. Students then have the opportunity to take their own research and present it to school administration or local school boards with consideration to school bullying and gun control policies. Particularly in light of the most recent school shooting in Parkland, Florida, and students' responses throughout the country, students can use this opportunity to reflect on how they can affect change.

Media Portrayal

After reading *Mockingbird*, teachers and students can discuss how nonprint texts, namely popular TV shows, have addressed school shootings and their impact. In order to facilitate such discussions, classes may pay particular attention to TV shows such as *One Tree Hill* (2006), *Degrassi* (2004), *7th Heaven* (1998), *Glee* (2013), *and Criminal Minds* (2011).

Students should be encouraged to reflect on the theatrical choices each episode made. For example, a teacher might ask the following questions:

- Was the actual shooting shown or implied?
- How was the shooter portrayed?

- How did the director draw attention to the victims' physical and emotional pain?
- If/how was the shooting addressed in future episodes?
- If/how actors/actresses spoke out about the episode?

Based on their analysis of the episode, students can argue for the purpose of the shooting in the episode: an actor/director's desire to take a stance on a current issue, in response to a current tragedy, to attract viewers or media attention, or to develop significant plot or character development.

Unsurprisingly, these episodes sparked conversations among fans and non-viewers alike, which secondary students can analyze rhetorically. Students may further consider public outcry over the media portrayal of school shootings and compare/contrast adults' commentary to the commentary of young viewers on social media sites such as Twitter and Reddit.

After watching and analyzing the film clips as well as the public's reactions, students can write their own responses to the shows in the form of an op-ed. Using mentor texts from credible sources such as the *Washington Post* or the *New York Times*, students should write about the positive or negative impact such shows can have on teenagers. As such, students will be able to develop their own voice and stance while synthesizing evidence and counter-arguments. The class may further elect to partner with their school's newspaper to publish or reach out to the local news to disseminate in print or online.

CAUTIONS AND ADVICE

This text deals with not only the effects of a mass school shooting but also the personal loss of a family member due to both gun violence and cancer. Moreover, given the rise of mass shootings across America, Kathryn Erskine's (2012) *Mockingbird* merits thoughtful attention in the secondary classroom; at the same time, teachers must be particularly mindful of how the text may directly affect their students. Teachers are called to know their community as well as their individual students before beginning this text.

Teachers are encouraged to develop prereading conversations that signal the tragedies that occur in this novel. Teachers may also consider working with their guidance counselors to facilitate conversations in their classrooms especially if such a tragedy has occurred within their community.

CONCLUSION

Kathryn Erskine's (2012) *Mockingbird* resonates with younger and older secondary students alike. The raw emotion and grief Caitlin experiences draws readers into the text and allows readers to experience the range of ways people can cope with the same tragic event. Moreover, this novel encourages readers to consider the ways in which finding closure is a journey as opposed to a singular event.

Beyond the pages of the text, readers are called to ponder the ways in which individuals and communities must together seek closure. Inspired readers may even further ponder these themes to consider the underlying causes and lasting impacts of grief and coping as well as school shootings. Largely due to the text's apparent simplicity, this novel invites all readers to slow down and reflect deeply on the novel's message of community support as well as individual grief and hope.

BOX 7.2 CONNECTED RESOURCES

Doyne, S. (2018, February 20). Can high school students make a real impact on the problem of gun violence in the United States? *New York Times*. Retrieved from https://www.nytimes.com/2018/02/20/ learning/can-high-school-students-make-a-real-impact-on-the-prob lem-of-gun-violence-in-the-united-states.html

In this *NY Times* piece, students and teachers alike can consider the impact teenagers across the United States have had in light of the 2018 Parkland school shooting.

Gallagher, K. (2018, February 21). Mass shooting unit: Day 1 [Blog post]. Retrieved from http://www.kellygallagher.org/kellys-blog/ mass-shooting-unit-day-1

Kelly Gallagher has created a twelve-day lesson play in response to the 2018 Parkland School Shooting, which allows students to create their own argumentative writing piece.

American School Counselor Association. (2018). Helping kids after a shooting. Retrieved from https://www.schoolcounselor.org/school-counselors/ professional-development/learn-more/shooting-resources

Compiled by the American School Counselor Association, this resource provides teachers with a variety of tools and articles about how to address school shootings with students.

REFERENCES

Aronofsky, D. (Producer), & Larrain, P. (Director). (2016). *Jackie* [Motion picture]. United States: Fox Searchlight Pictures.

Beers, G. K., & Probst, R. E. (2017). *Disrupting thinking: Why how we read matters.* New York, NY: Scholastic.

Buehler, J. (2016). *Teaching reading with YA literature: Complex texts, complex lives.* Urbana, IL: National Council of Teachers of English.

Erskine, K. (2012). *Mockingbird.* London, UK: Usborne Books.

Everytown for Gun Safety Support Fund. (2018). 306 shootings in America since 2013. Retrieved from https://everytownresearch.org/school-shootings/

Frazier, B. (Writer), & Teng, L. (Director). (2011). Painless [Television series episode]. In G. Coello-Bannon & H. V. Bring (Producers), *Criminal minds.* Santa Monica, CA: CBS Television Distribution.

Hampton, B. (Writer), & Inch, K. (Director). (1998). Johnny get your gun [Television series episode]. In Brinckerhoff, B. (Producer), *7th Heaven.* Los Angeles, CA: Spelling Television.

Hodgson, M. (Writer), & Buecker, B. (Director). (2013). Shooting Star [Television series episode]. In R. Murphy, B. Falchuk, & I. Brennan (Producers), *Glee.* Hollywood, Los Angeles, CA: Paramount Studios.

Lee, H. (1960). *To kill a mockingbird.* New York, NY: Hachette.

Prange, G. (Writer), & Schwahn, M. (Director). (2006). With tired eyes, tired minds, tired souls, we slept [Television series episode]. In J. Davola (Producer), *One tree hill.* Burbank, CA: Warner Brothers Television.

Schuyler, L. (Writer), & Scaini, S. (Director). (2004). Time stands still: Part 1 [Television series episode]. In A. Martin, L. Schuyler, E. Schwarzman, & S. Stohn (Producers), *Degrassi: The next generation.* Toronto, ON: Entertainment One.

Schuyler, L. (Writer), & Scaini, S. (Director). (2004). Time stands still: Part 2 [Television series episode]. In A. Martin, L. Schuyler, E. Schwarzman, & S. Stohn (Producers), *Degrassi: The next generation.* Toronto, ON: Entertainment One.

Chapter 8

This Is Where It Ends: How Studying School Shootings from Multiple Perspectives Promotes Critical Literacy

Shelly Shaffer, Amye Ellsworth,
and Kellie Crawford

"Since 2013, there have been over 200 school shootings in America—an average of nearly one a week" (Everytown for Gun Safety Support Fund, 2018). School violence in the form of school shootings is a tragedy that too often affects the lives of students in the United States. As a result, educators must face this difficult issue but may struggle to find effective strategies to discuss this type of death and violence in their classroom.

When young adult (YA) authors write stories of school shootings, they often explore many different perspectives, including survivors' perspectives, the accounts of family members of either the shooter or the victims, or even the shooter's viewpoint. This chapter provides entry into discussions around how reading a YA book dealing with the topic of school shootings can help readers to examine mass shootings and gain insight into this grim phenomenon.

Several activities that focus on thinking, talking, and writing about the topic of death are included in the chapter, all of which address literacy standards. These activities and strategies provide English language arts (ELA) teachers with tools to facilitate lessons on school shootings while developing critical literacy and empathy in young people, as per Lewison, Flint, and Van Sluys (2002).

Lewison, Flint, and Van Sluys (2002) identified four dimensions of critical literacy: "(1) disrupting the commonplace, (2) interrogating multiple viewpoints, (3) focusing on sociopolitical issues, and (4) taking action and promoting social justice" (p. 362). These four dimensions are addressed in the unit included in this chapter.

Scorza, Mirra, and Morell (2013) suggest critical pedagogy empowers youth to understand and articulate relationships between power, dominance, and hegemony. The authors claim by learning to use critical literacy to analyze the world around them, learners can make "more empowered choices as individuals and democratic participants;" as a result of critical pedagogy, "are [students] reading the word and the world in more powerful ways?" (p. 23). Marin and Halpern (2011) found that teaching critical thinking explicitly is the most effective way for young people to develop critical-thinking skills.

In this chapter, the activities scaffold critical-thinking abilities. Some suggestions of activities presented in this chapter include using an anticipation guide, creating "tea party" roles (Christensen, 2000), reading multiple supporting texts, completing a graphic organizer, and writing poems and an editorial based on the text and personal experiences.

Park (2012) suggests, "Through critical literacy, people can generate deeper and different understandings of texts; question social and economic realities; and reimagine the status quo" (p. 630). Learners develop broader awareness of the many factors that affect (and are affected by) school shootings by reading texts that discuss death through a critical lens.

SUMMARY OF *THIS IS WHERE IT ENDS*

This Is Where It Ends (Nijkamp, 2016) tells the story of a mass shooting at Opportunity High School. The shooting is committed by Tyler Browne, the older brother of one of the main characters. The book includes text messages and online blog posts from several characters, as well as prose written from four main characters' perspectives.

The story begins at 10:01–10:02 A.M. with Claire and as the book continues, the author provides timestamps for readers at the beginning of each chapter. At 10:05–10:07 A.M., the shooting starts. As the principal finishes her welcome speech, Tyler takes the stage and the audience soon realizes the doors have been locked. Brandishing a gun, Tyler forces his captive audience to listen, and pay for their perceived crimes.

Using the book *This Is Where It Ends* to study the topic of school shootings can promote critical literacy in the ELA classroom due to the author's use of multiple perspectives. The book's four main characters, Tomás, Sylv, Claire, and Autumn, provide the readers with insight into how a school shooting can transform a community.

Claire is the shooter's ex-girlfriend, and her character complicates the relationship that people have with perpetrators of crimes; Claire still cares about Tyler and cannot believe that he is capable of such heinous actions. Autumn is Tyler's baby sister, and readers are torn when Autumn's character who, while horrified by her brother's viciousness, also tells him, "I love you. . . . You're my brother. You're my best friend" (p. 146).

Autumn's character demonstrates the complex relationship she has with her brother, and this revelation causes readers to sympathize not only with Autumn but also with her brother Tyler as well. Tomás and Sylv are twins whose relationships with both Autumn and Tyler put them in the middle of the devastation taking place in the school auditorium. All of these perspectives provide YA readers in an ELA classroom with multiple ways to scrutinize the same event and to develop insight not only into causes of the crime but also into how crimes affect people.

PROMOTING CRITICAL LITERACY IN *THIS IS WHERE IT ENDS*

Thinking, reading, and writing about traumatic events develop YAs' critical literacy. *This Is Where It Ends* offers many different perspectives, and careful examination of these perspectives provides important insight into trauma suffered by perpetrators, victims, and survivors of school violence. Pre-, during-, and postreading activities guide learners through a unit using the novel *This Is Where It Ends*. Activities include using an anticipation guide, multiple texts, and a graphic organizer; developing roles that examine the various characters; and writing to engage in the numerous interpretations of the event.

Preparing Young People to Engage with Difficult Texts and Topics

Before beginning the novel, students perform activities that facilitate engagement with the text. Completing an anticipation guide and reading a nonfiction excerpt provides background information on the themes the book discusses and participating in a "tea party" (Christensen, 2000) activity develops interest in the characters of the book prior to reading.

Anticipation Guide

Since the topic of school shootings is one that has touched the lives of so many educators and young people, the introduction of this topic should be done in a considerate and responsible way. One way to introduce difficult topics into class discussion is through an anticipation guide. According to Gunning (2008), the anticipation guide strategy is an effective instructional technique that assists in activating prior knowledge, making predictions, analyzing understandings of ideas and beliefs, and confronting and clarifying misconceptions of concepts and beliefs.

Anticipation guides in secondary classrooms have traditionally been completed on paper during class. They include five to ten controversial statements relating to the text, asking students to respond to each statement by giving an opinion on a scale or by writing a sentence, thus facilitating discussion.

With new technology available in many classrooms, anticipation guides can now be administered online and then discussed during class, with learners accessing the anticipation guide through their personal devices or classroom computers. Using technology allows the teacher to access data from the entire class' anticipation guide responses and to display charts of the responses during the discussion.

For *This Is Where It Ends*, the anticipation guide questions are available through a Google form to be completed during the first few minutes of class. The anticipation guide included in this chapter (see table 8.1) would be adapted to a Google form to complete online.

Following the completion of the anticipation guide, the teacher displays the Google form results with the corresponding questions on the projector for discussion.

Table 8.1.   Anticipation Guide: *This Is Where It Ends*

Directions: Read each statement and rank it. After rating each statement, choose one of the statements and write a short paragraph (seven to ten sentences) explaining why you have that opinion.

	Strongly Disagree	Disagree	Agree	Strongly Agree
People should stand up for those who are bullied.				
Perpetrators of crimes are evil people.				
I would never be able to forgive somebody for hurting my family.				
Guns should be more regulated in the United States.				
Access to guns causes most of the violence in the United States to happen.				
School shootings are random acts of violence.				
Teachers and principals should be armed.				
We can prevent school shootings.				
I would still love my family member if he or she hurt somebody else.				

After the anticipation guide, the students read an excerpt from the nonfiction text *Rampage: The Social Roots of School Shootings* (see box 8.1). Chapter 3, "Explaining Rampage School Shootings" (pp. 47–73), provides some research and context for school shootings, including popular explanations of why these events continue to occur.

Working with groups, each group presents one of the popular explanations of school shootings to share with the class; topics include mental illness, "he just snapped," family problems, bullying, peer support, changing communities, culture of violence, gun availability, violent media, and the copycat effect. During the ensuing discussion, each of the explanations will be ranked in order from most to least blame for school shootings.

Both the anticipation guide and nonfiction excerpts offer background on the themes encountered while reading the book. Students formulate and share opinions, while also learning about themes related to school shootings. This pair of activities also provides a foundation for discussion regarding the upcoming novel.

Tea Party

After establishing background for the book by exploring themes, students become acquainted with the novel itself. More engagement will be developed by introducing the text in an exciting way. Prior to reading the text, the teacher prepares "Tea Party" roles for each of the main characters, as per Christensen (2000). *This Is Where It Ends* has four primary characters that can be used for the tea party roles although the teacher could also prepare additional roles for Tyler and other characters from the text.

Christensen's (2000) tea party moves beyond a simple book talk, providing the opportunity to make predictions about each character and explore key ideas from the book prior to reading. This kind of introduction to the text presents opportunities for critical thinking before even beginning the text.

Students make predictions and inferences and write questions about the characters in the text through the brief introductions to each of the characters they experience through the tea party activity. Prepared by the teacher ahead of time using excerpts from the text or by writing summaries of each character, the tea party works best when multiple viewpoints are available in the text.

During the class activity, students read their own roles and "meet" other characters from the book, which develops interest in the book. Chapter 1 of *This Is Where It Ends* (pp. 1–8) includes each of the main characters' points of view, and excerpts from this first chapter can be used for the tea party roles. Suggested tea party roles for *This Is Where It Ends* are included in table 8.2.

Assign each student one tea party role to perform. The learners carefully read the role they have received, making notes about the person's character

Table 8.2. Tea Party Roles

Claire	Tomás	Autumn	Sylv
"Track season starts in a couple weeks, but no one has told Coach Lindt about winter. He's convinced that the only way to get us into shape is to practice—even when my breath freezes right in front of me. This is Opportunity, Alabama. Sane people don't leave their homes while it's white and frosty outside. . . . Still, Coach Lindt's start-of-season training beats Principal Trenton's long and arduous start-of-semester speech—virtue, hard work, and the proper behavior of young ladies and gentlemen. Almost four years at Opportunity High, I can recite her words from memory, which is exactly what I did for Matt at breakfast this morning-responsibility, opportunity ('no pun intended'), and her favorite, our school motto, *We Shape the Future*. It sounds glorious, but with months left until graduation, I have no clue what the future looks like. If Opportunity shaped me, I didn't notice. Running, I know. This track, I know. One step after another after another. It doesn't matter what comes next as long as I keep moving forward. My foot slips, and I stumble" (pp. 1–2).	"Time's up. The small clock on the bookshelf strikes ten with an annoying little tune, and I thumb through the tabs in front of me at supersonic speed. *C'mon, c'mon, c'mon.* It only took superglue—strategically squirted on the desk drawers of my favorite Spanish teacher, Mr. Look-At-Me-Strutting-My-Stuff-Like-A-Walking-Midlife-Crisis—for Far and me to find our way to the administrative office. But it took both our student IDs before we managed to jiggle the lock on Principal Trenton's door. And it'll all be for nothing if I can't find the file I'm looking for. . . . Fareed rolls his eyes and gestures for me to keep quiet. *Someone's in the hallway,* he mouths. He tiptoes back to the door. *Crap.* How do I explain this?" (pp. 3–4).	"Here at Opportunity, we pride ourselves in shaping the doctors, lawyers, and politicians of tomorrow.' Trenton holds the microphone loosely while she scans the crowd, as if memorizing every single face. So many students come and go, leaving nothing but the faintest impression, names scratched into desks and graffitied onto bathroom stalls, yet she knows us all. All our hopes. All our heartbreaks. All our sleepless nights. Her eyes linger on me, and my neck burns. I reach for the chair to my right, but it remains as it was when the assembly started. Empty. To my left, Sylv groans. . . . In truth Sylv will have plenty of colleges to choose from. She's a shoo-in for all her dream schools. And I should be happy for her. I *am* happy for her. But for me, college is the only way out of this misery, and Dad sure as hell isn't going to pay for my ride. Not to study dance. 'Look what happened to your mother,' he'd say. I grip my crumpled coffee cup, grab the threadbare denim messenger bag under my seat, and block out Ty's voice in the back of my mind. My brother would tell me that Principal Trenton's words are truer than I think, that the world is at my fingertips and it's up to me to make my future the best it can be" (pp. 5–6).	"I sink deep into my seat and glance at the empty place next to Autumn. He's not coming after all. He'd have been here by now. He won't come. I'm safe here. *He won't come.* The knot in my stomach unfurls and recoils with every twist and turn of my mind. I could ask Autumn about Tyler, but she's lost in memories. Today is two years since the accident. She refuses to share her grief with me—or anyone. Even when she smiles, she isn't the girl she used to be. And I miss her. Some days, when she thinks no one is watching, she still moves across the floor as if she's flying. . . . Instead, it's another Monday. Life goes one. The assembly is over, and Autumn holds herself ramrod straight. I'm the only one who knows she'll fly out of this cage and leave us all behind as soon as she can" (p. 7).

traits and other important facts, and writing two to three questions they have about their character after reading the excerpt. Getting up and roaming the classroom to meet the other three characters from the text is the next step in the process. Once they encounter another character, they write his or her name down and write notes or a description of the character as the other person introduces him or herself.

Once each student has had a chance to be introduced to the other characters, they return to their seats and generate a visual representation that shows connections they have been able to make. Park (2012) found that visualization was an effective strategy for developing critical literacy. After the activity, students share questions and predictions they have about the characters in the book.

Multiple Texts and Multiple Characters Facilitate Critical Reading

Reading this book provides the opportunity for the analysis of how a school shooting affects the characters in the text. By approaching this book through a critical lens, students examine characters in ways that encourage readers to step into each character's shoes, including the shooter himself and to transact with the text, as suggested by Rosenblatt (1995).

Multiple Texts

To aid in the development of critical perspectives, nonfiction texts, other fiction texts, and multimedia texts will be incorporated in the unit. The examination of multiple texts dealing with the same topic is mentioned in ELA standards, which ask learners to consider how multiple texts address similar ideas and themes.

In addition to the text from *This Is Where It Ends,* supplementary texts can support the critical exploration of issues in the unit. These resources include songs, video clips, excerpts from fiction and nonfiction texts, and poems (see box 8.1). Each additional text will be paired with the novel, and discussion will take place after reading or viewing each. Investigation and comparison of the topic of school shootings from the various perspectives presented and the novel itself can occur through reading supporting texts.

Each of the accompanying texts will be incorporated into the unit at key times in the novel. For example, "There Has Been a Shooting at Columbine High School" (see box 8.1) will be read and discussed as news of the shooting spreads throughout the town of Opportunity in *This Is Where It Ends.* The excerpt (from the book *A Mother's Reckoning: Living the Aftermath of Tragedy*) tells the true account of Columbine shooter, Dylan Klebold's mother, Sue, as she first heard the news of the shooting at Columbine.

Along with the text, news reports from the Columbine and the Sandy Hook School shootings (see box 8.1) will be viewed. Watching these news reports helps students to imagine the chaos and vulnerability characters in the novel experience as the tragedy of the shooting unfolds. Each of these texts supports critical literacy by aiding visualization of the events from multiple perspectives (Park, 2012). Thinking about how school shootings affect the community at large, they can also consider how these tragedies affect the families of both the victims and the shooters.

Character Chart

A chart about the main characters, Tomás, Sylv, Claire, Autumn, and Tyler, will be completed while reading. The chart includes categories for each character's name; main characteristics, including strengths and weaknesses; connections between other characters; and ways the shooting affects each character.

This activity addresses ELA standards by asking learners to use textual evidence to support claims, including making inferences or by citing the text explicitly. The teacher asks students to stop at the end of chapters to meet with small groups to complete individual characterization charts, and as sharing and discussion of these characteristics takes place, a class chart will also be produced.

Each of these characters provides a view of the shooting that young people may not have considered: a student outside the school who is safe, but helpless; a brother inside the school, but outside of the auditorium; a sister inside the auditorium, who is afraid of the shooter; the sister of the shooter, who wants to stop her brother from hurting more people; and the shooter himself. Students not only examine multiple perspectives from a powerful text on a school shooting, they also form personal connections between themselves and the characters, as per Rosenblatt (1995).

Writing to Develop Critical Literacy

To follow up the novel, the critical study of the characters in the text that was developed while reading will be used to write both a narrative and an argumentative piece. By incorporating two types of writing, students will be able to analyze a character with a found poem that uses the text itself to demonstrate understanding and to wrestle with a difficult theme and assume the role of one of the characters in an editorial, both of which will develop Lewison Flint, and Van Sluys' (2002) dimensions of critical literacy even further.

Editorial

After reading the novel, one of the major themes from the novel will be chosen as the focus to write an editorial. The teacher will provide models of editorials for students to read and use as they write their own. The novel and the supplementary texts read throughout the unit will support their opinions through the use of textual evidence.

The editorial can be based on one of the anticipation guide statements or on another idea. The assignment will take the form of a RAFT, a writing assignment in which the writing prompt includes the Role, Audience, Format, Topic (Groenke & Puckett, 2006).

Students will write the editorial from the point of view of somebody from the novel: a main character, a newspaper reporter, police officer, concerned citizen, or another point of view. Editorials will be published in a class newspaper. This assignment moves young people into an active role as a "citizen" in the community of the shooting. By imagining themselves as part of the community in which the school shooting occurred, they consider how a school shooting would affect their own lives.

Poetry

Once students have read the text and thoroughly explored each character, they will be assigned one of the characters from the book as the basis for a found poem. Small groups will be formed based on characters from the novel. The topic of the poem will be: "How did your character experience loss?" The students discuss the topic of the poem with their small group and use the book and their character charts to write a collaborative found poem based on that character's experiences in the novel. The poems, based on the five main characters, will be shared with the class and displayed.

To end this lesson, students write individual poems about loss. The class will watch "Shooter" (see box 8.1), a slam poetry performance about a school shooting to promote thinking about their own poems.

Students will use the praise, question, polish (PQP) strategy (Neubert & NcNelis, 1990) to evaluate the poem and then will be encouraged to write from their heart (Nelson, 1998). They can take a line or an idea from "Shooter" to get started or write their own, choosing to write as vulnerably and openly as they feel comfortable. An opportunity will be provided to share poems during a slam poetry performance.

CAUTIONS AND ADVICE

When teachers decide to include a novel, such as *This Is Where It Ends* in their curriculum, they will need to be prepared for the difficult conversations that are bound to arise. Factors in and out of school (recent deaths from gun violence, recent shootings/lockdowns, sensitivity about issues surrounding gun control) may affect receptivity to discussing the topic; however, as documented after the school shooting in Parkland, Florida, in February 2018, students want to talk about the issue and take a stand (Miller, 2018; Nguyen, 2018).

While educators may feel the need to protect young people from harsh truths, what we see in these situations is that they are the ones demanding discussion. They want to talk about the issues; they want to take a stand; they want to make a difference.

Teachers can promote this by creating an environment in the classroom where it is safe to talk about difficult topics and examine the many factors that surround these issues. By constructing a safe space in your classroom, and by making allies in the community (Fleischer, 2017), educators can promote social justice and advocacy in their classrooms by being brave enough to bring difficult topics into the classroom and facilitating these conversations.

CONCLUSION

Bringing texts about school shootings and gun violence into the ELA classrooms can be daunting for teachers; however, the choice to not incorporate texts that deal with this difficult issue means that discussion and critical thinking about school shootings will not occur. These discussions benefit students by developing understanding and empathy of these terrible events.

Closely reading texts that present multiple viewpoints of school shootings is helpful for developing critical literacy; the YA book discussed in this chapter will provide an opportunity for young people to think critically about death in a way that nonfiction and informational texts do not. Placing themselves in the shoes of those with divergent experiences and viewpoints increases empathy and teaches how to understand and overcome prejudices. Each of the activities presented in this chapter will provide a framework for the type of critical-thinking ELA teachers are called on to develop in our students.

BOX 8.1   CONNECTED RESOURCES

ABC News. (1999, April 20). *Columbine shooting* [Video file]. Retrieved from http://abcnews.go.com/Archives/video/april-20-1999-columbine-shooting-9541833

CNN. (2012, December 14). *20 children killed in school shooting* [Video file]. Retrieved from https://www.cnn.com/videos/bestoftv/2012/12/14/exp-erin-ashleigh-banfield-reports-on-sandy-hook-elementary-school-shooting.cnn

The news videos from CNN and ABC News will be used to help students to visualize the chaos and vulnerability characters in the novel experience as the tragedy of the shooting unfolds. Survivor accounts and reporting from immediately after the shooting will give students an unfiltered look at how real-life counterparts to Nijkamp's characters reacted to the school shooting.

Deviller, D., Hosein, S., & Kipner, S. (2002). Stole [Recorded by K. Rowland]. On *simply deep* [CD]. Los Angeles, CA: Columbia.

The song "Stole" will be paired with an excerpt from *This Is Where It Ends*. In "Stole," Kelly Rowland introduces us to three high school students whose lives were destroyed by different forms of gun violence. This song would be an excellent hook point of view (POV).

Klebold, S. (2016). *A mother's reckoning: Living in the aftermath of tragedy*. New York, NY: Crown Publishing.

An excerpt from this book will be read and discussed as news of the shooting spreads throughout the town of Opportunity in *This Is Where It Ends*. The excerpt is from the perspective of Sue Klebold, the mother of Dylan Klebold, one of the Columbine Shooters.

Newman, K. S., Fox, C., Harding, D., Mehta, J., & Roth, W. (2004). *Rampage: The social roots of school shootings*. New York, NY: Basic Books.

This book provides background information about school shootings. After completing the anticipation guide, students will discuss research-based motives attributed to school shootings. This text excerpt provides excellent background information.

Siskeljacobs. (2013, June 3). *"Shooter"—Lamar Jorden* [Video file]. Retrieved from https://www.youtube.com/watch?v=Dfqwv-l1HXk

As students watch the raw emotion and vulnerability of Lamar Jorden's slam poetry performance, they will be inspired and encouraged to write their own poems about loss based upon their POV studies of the novel's characters.

REFERENCES

Everytown for Gun Safety Support Fund. (2018). *Analysis of school shootings.* Retrieved from https://everytownresearch.org/reports/analysis-of-school-shootings/

Fleischer, C. (2017). Creating a safer environment for change. *Voice from the Middle, 25*(2), 44–46.

Groenke, S. L., & Puckett, R. (2006). Becoming environmentally literate citizens: Students use the RAFT writing strategy to address land development issues. *Science Teacher, 73*(8), 22–27.

Gunning, T. G. (2008). *Creating literacy instruction for all students* (6th ed.). New York, NY: Pearson.

Lewison, M., Flint, A. S., & Van Sluys, K. (2002). Taking on critical literacy: The journey of newcomers and novices. *Language Arts, 79*(5), 382–92.

Marin, L. M., & Halpern, D. F. (2011). Pedagogy for developing critical thinking in adolescents: Explicit instruction produces greatest gains. *Thinking Skills and Creativity, 6*(1), 1–13.

Miller, S. (2018, February 18). We will be the last mass shooting: Florida students want to be tipping point in gun debate. *USA Today.* Retrieved from https://www.usatoday.com/story/news/nation/2018/02/17/we-last-mass-shooting-florida-students-might-tipping-point-gun-debate/347992002/

Nelson, G. L. (1998). Writing from the feather circle: Seeking a "language of that different yield." *The Quarterly, 20*(3), 5–9.

Neubert, G. A., & McNelis, S. J. (1990). Peer response: Teaching specific revision suggestions. *English Journal, 79*(5), 52–56.

Nijkamp, M. (2016). *This is where it ends.* Naperville, IL: Sourcebooks.

Nguyen, T. (2018, February 19). How the Parkland shooting survivors are trying to force Trump's hand. *Vanity Fair.* Retrieved from https://www.vanityfair.com/news/2018/02/parkland-shooting-survivors-gun-control-protests

Rosenblatt, L. M. (1995). *Literature as exploration* (5th ed.). New York, NY: Modern Language Association of America.

Scorza, D., Mirra, N., & Morell, E. (2013). It should just be education: Critical pedagogy normalized as academic excellence. *International Journal of Critical Pedagogy, 4*(2), 15–34.

Chapter 9

Graphic Young Adult Literature Representations of Brutalized Communities: Exploring Loss through Don Brown's *Drowned City: Hurricane Katrina & New Orleans*

Shelbie Witte and Jennifer S. Dail

Five months after Hurricane Katrina hit, we all came back to school. It was surreal: not every building had running water and electricity, many parts of the campus were still uninhabitable—it was clear that our new normal was anything but. And so there I was standing in front of a group of students who had collectively lost so much. Students lost family members, homes, their past. I didn't know if I had the strength, or the ability, to get them to see the value of what we were doing in the classroom. How do I create an authentic space of learning when survival was what we were mostly doing? I think this moment forced me to forget about everything but what mattered most: the students. And this is something that I still take with me today. Disasters teach us about humanity, and our resilience, our empathy: and our compassion; this is what we focused on and wrote about in the classroom.

—Kelly Thayer, personal communication (January 16, 2018)

Teachers cannot avoid death and loss as topics in their English language arts (ELA) classrooms. Frequently acknowledged representations of death in the ELA classroom occur not only in the canonical and young adult novels teachers love to share with students but also through the lived lives of students as they inevitably face death through the loss of acquaintances, classmates, close friends, pets, or family members. Death impacts students profoundly, which is why the topic deserves space for conversation in ELA classrooms.

While some teachers approach the topic of death head-on, inviting adolescents to share their experiences and questions, others are more hesitant to discuss it in any form or fashion, creating an "elephant in the room" that all know are there, but are unwilling to acknowledge. This chapter explores how teachers might talk about death in brutalized communities through using graphic young adult literature (YAL) representations.

Brutalized communities defined as those where events, whether natural or manmade and beyond their control, impact the citizens' circumstances and bring widespread premature death to members of the community. Historical examples of this include the Holocaust, Japanese internment during World War II, genocide in Rwanda, and the effects of hurricanes such as the recent Irma and Maria. In this chapter, graphic YAL representations of Hurricane Katrina will be examined through the book *Drowned City: Hurricane Katrina & New Orleans* (Brown, 2015).

Drowned City shows issues of oppression and brutalization, helping students better recognize the brutalities in the world in which they live and allows them to explore those issues, including the death that results from these events. The death in *Drowned City* is not a human-made act like genocide; it is a natural disaster. Examining death through a natural disaster such as Hurricane Katrina helps students consider social responsibility in their communities and the responses to these disasters and people affected by them. Additional themes such as racism, emergency preparedness, and even larger social justice umbrella topics can be explored.

Graphic novels are still finding their way into mainstream ELA classrooms; yet, they offer unique possibilities for representing events and facilitating discussion about those events. In the world of social media and instant news, teachers and students are inundated with images of brutalized communities on a daily basis. Graphic novels represent those images through illustrations, creating some distance between the reader and the event, which will enable students to discuss the effects of these events in a more authentic, less desensitized manner.

Graphic novels also support students' literacy beyond print-centric texts. Graphic novels have an imbedded scaffold that points to what students know and supports students extending new knowledge, building upon already existing reading skills, especially inference, given the students' reliance on images over text.

SUMMARY OF *DROWNED CITY: HURRICANE KATRINA & NEW ORLEANS*

Drowned City: Hurricane Katrina & New Orleans (2015) is a short graphic novel that explores the loss and brutality that Hurricane Katrina unleashed on the city of New Orleans in August 2005. In the hurricane, 80 percent of the city of New Orleans was flooded. Property damage was in the hundreds of billions of dollars, and more than 1,400 people lost their lives. Others were displaced as they moved what—if any—remaining belongings they had to new cities.

While disaster organizations such as Federal Emergency Management Agency (FEMA) and individuals volunteered their time to help those in the brutalized community of New Orleans, people, including trusted officials such as police officers, looted the city's businesses, further adding to the brutalization in the community. The African-American community was hit hardest by Hurricane Katrina, making this natural disaster a trigger for exponentially highlighting the racial divides within the United States as well as the lack of preparedness on behalf of the federal and local government agency to respond to a disaster of this size.

The images Brown (2015) presents in this text are kinetic, meaning they depend "upon movement for [their] effects" (The Art Story Foundation, 2017). These images engage readers as they depict the movement of the people and the storm. In contrast, realistic depictions detract from the reader's ability to make meaning (McCloud, 1994).

Brown (2015) varies the framing on the pages to help portray that movement. For example, when victims arrived at the Superdome on August 31 to discover that it was locked at not accepting any more people, the frame spans two pages where one and a quarter of them are filled with shoulder-to-shoulder people outside the Superdome (Brown, 2015, pp. 60–61).

The vast frame shows the size of the crowd that was turned away and the crowding and desperation those seeking shelter felt. In contrast, as the hurricane rolled into the shore of Buras, Louisiana, the frames still span two pages, but are layered in four horizontal frames showing the Gulf of Mexico on the left side as it invades the frame on the right side to hit land (Brown, 2015, pp. 14–15). The layout shows how the sea water invaded the land and crossed the imaginary barrier between sea and land as depicted by the fold in the page.

The novel also represents death and trauma clearly in the images, focusing not just on people but on affected animals as well. For example, as the levee breaches grew and canal floodwalls developed holes, Brown (2015) shows a person hip-deep in water carrying his bag on his head and a dog alongside him (p. 48). Fish visibly swim in this newly released water.

As the waters grow more stagnant and black, however, fish are dying, and a frame depicts that by showing some floating belly-up in darker water (Brown, 2015, p. 49). When people are using boats to escape their homes in the flooding waters, readers see frames with insects such as mosquitos and gnats swarming around people and even poisonous snakes in the water (Brown, 2015, p. 41).

PERSPECTIVE TAKING WITH *DROWNED CITY*

A central practice in studying literature is helping students adopt different perspectives about characters, and events. Part of this perspective taking is examining the role that characters play in a drama (Beach, Appleman, Hynds, & Wilhelm, 2006). In the context of *Drowned City*, students examine the role that ideological or institutional organizations play in responding to natural disasters like Hurricane Katrina. Students can better partake in perspective taking when they form connections between the literature and life and are able to elaborate on the story world (Wilhelm, 2016).

Using character perspectives to study literature will help students develop empathy for real-world events and people, not just those represented in the story world. In developing empathy in students, teachers often have the goal of creating more responsible citizens in their students—citizens who take care of people and the world in which they live. These principles guide the approaches proposed here for teaching this text as part of conversation about death in the ELA classroom.

Questions to Guide Studying Death through *Drowned City*

Students benefit from questions that facilitate deep, meaningful in-class conversation, especially when the novel deals with sensitive subjects such as death. Socratic Circles (Copeland, 2005) provide opportunities for students to explore controversial topics in a student-centered format, as students ask questions of one another independently with limited teacher support. If students need prompts to move discussions forward, following are some questions to use in discussing the entire novel. These are probing questions that ask students to draw causal connections between events depicted in the book.

- What actions led to the overall catastrophic impact of Hurricane Katrina on the city of New Orleans?
- How did the events of Hurricane Katrina affect the people of New Orleans?
- What communities were most impacted? In what ways?
- Where are examples of humanity illustrated in this book? Provide examples.
- Where are examples of inhumanity illustrated in this book? Provide examples.

- What circumstances existed to cause the loss of 1,400 people? Could the circumstances have been changed prevented?
- What could have been done differently to prevent such a high number of deaths?
- What could have been done differently to better serve the survivors of this disaster?

In addition to these questions, teachers should use the opportunity for students to develop and ask their own questions and explore possible answers or solutions for the questions they encounter as they read.

Scenario-Based Response

Scenario-based responses are an authentic way to engage students with the ideas presented in texts, asking them to assume a role and respond from that perspective. This text lends itself well to asking students to craft a scenario-based response. Scenario-based responses often call for additional research on the part of students, as well, making this a good opportunity to point students toward their own community and resources (NCTE & IRA, 2012). Here is a possible scenario for use with this graphic novel:

- Imagine you are running for the office of mayor in the wake a large-scale natural disaster in your city. People have not yet had the chance to start rebuilding their homes or their lives, and some have not even been able to return to the city. Morale and trust are both low, and people are looking for new leadership. Write a speech or public advertisement you will give as part of your campaign for mayor. How will you make life better for people? What steps will you implement to help them rebuild? Who will you need to partner with in the community to help accomplish these actions?

While discussing death is not implicit in this activity, it guides students to consider how individuals and communities move forward following disasters and loss. Focusing on the steps needed to move forward, this scenario requires students to consider the impact of a disaster from multiple perspectives as well as critically consider how to best leverage the resources of a community for those most in need.

In addition to the aforementioned discussion and scenario role-play, teachers can use the opportunity to weave visual literacy strategies into the reading of the graphic novel, as it is rich in opportunities to critically engage with print and no-print depictions of loss.

Instructional Strategy #1: Creating Narrative with Visual Frames

This is a prereading strategy to use with students when reading graphic novels. In short, small groups of students receive a selected set of frames that do not contain text and are asked to read the images, sequence them, and create a narrative around those images. For this to be most effective, do not introduce the novel or let students know which text it came from until after the activity. With the event of Hurricane Katrina, in particular, students may come with prior knowledge and preconceived notions about the disaster depending upon their experiences. The goal is to invite them to read the images without layering those outside ideas upon them.

Go through the graphic novel and select frames that have no text or copy frames and remove their text. Some good frames for use in *Drowned City* can be found on the following pages: 5, 19, 26, 31, 38, 47, 58, 72, and 87. While each of these pages may contain some text, it can easily be removed by cutting out the individual frames for students. Additionally, it is not necessarily recommended to use all of these exemplary frames as you don't want to give the whole story away to students.

Organize students into small groups and have them look at the images in their envelope. Ask students to read the images and consider if they see a possible story there. Encourage them to move them around and play with various sequences to see what makes the most sense to them in creating a story. After groups have had time to do this, have them share their sequences and stories back with the class, asking them to support their stories with evidence from the images.

Instructional Strategy #2: Reading Visual Images

This strategy could serve as either a prereading or early during-reading strategy for students. To successfully comprehend a graphic novel, students need to think about not just the words on the page but the images; however, the images are more than just the picture. In a graphic novel, they are intentionally framed and colored to convey meaning alongside the text.

For example, frames where the image pushes against some or all borders are conveying an idea around space. The character may be trying to push out of the space, or the space may not be large enough to contain the characters (see example from pages 60–61 mentioned previously). These are visual reading concepts teachers want to teach students so that they see the representations in graphic novels as conductors of meaning and more than cool pictures in the book.

Select different images from the book and spend time engaging students in reading them. Within this exploration of images, teachers might also need to give students some instruction in how to read a graphic novel: start at the upper-left corner and read across to the right, just as one would with a traditional novel. When reaching the end of the row, proceed down to the next row, and once at the bottom of the page, proceed across to the top-left corner of the next page and repeat. Some vocabulary students might need to be familiar with in reading these images are *panel* and *panel border* or *frame*.

Instructional Strategy #3: Critical Reading of News Media Texts

NCTE Standard 1 (2012) calls for students to read a wide range of print and nonprint texts in order to help them construct knowledge of themselves and the world in which they live. This strategy asks students to critically examine that world and put Hurricane Katrina in conversation with more recent natural disasters that have left communities brutalized. Critically reading media texts also belongs in the ELA classroom as part of this standard.

For this strategy, have students choose a natural disaster (recent ones include Hurricane Irma and its impact on Houston and Hurricane Maria and its impact on Puerto Rico) to research using credible news sources. There is a great deal of news stories currently available to research the readiness of response for disaster in the continental United States versus Puerto Rico in addition to the lack of response in Puerto Rico months after the disastrous hurricane. Have students examine and evaluate how media portrayed each event and create a comparison and contrast analysis of that coverage.

CAUTIONS AND ADVICE

Teachers truly never know the emotional baggage students carry with them when they come to school. Loss impacts each of us differently, as students especially struggle to navigate the complicated world of adolescence with brave faces. Emotional triggers such as death can make students feel uncomfortable and even unsafe in classrooms. While uncomfortable topics are not necessarily off-limits, a caution is that teachers must be prepared for a range of reactions to uncomfortable topics.

One recommendation is having a support system in place in advance of reading and engaging with difficult topics. Depending on the school structure, school counselors and school librarians can be excellent resources before, during, and after reading about controversial events and topics. School counselors especially may have resources to share about seeking help for grief counseling, depression, discrimination (e.g., racial and sexual), and other themes that emerge from discussions about the books students read.

Additionally, as students move into new school districts, teachers may not always know the circumstances surrounding those moves. Another recommendation is having an outlet for students to share their fears and concerns with trusted peers or adults in the school or classroom. Experience has shown that having an ongoing Issue Bin at the front of the class (a ballot box) allows students to put issues within the box anonymously in order to share with the teacher good news (celebrations) or concerns they have for the class, themselves, or a classmate.

CONCLUSION

> When life throws us in darkness, we have to find the light. And it's there--it just takes time, patience, and work to see it. Regardless of what obstacles, or disasters, occur in our lives, we have to fight to see the good.
>
> —Kelly Thayer, personal communication (January 16, 2018)

Schools and classrooms must be places where students can discuss their hopes and dreams as well as their fears and concerns. Unfortunately, teachers are sometimes faced with criticisms for either engaging in difficult, controversial conversations that makes students uncomfortable or being too frightened in having them at all, fearing approaching any topic that might draw attention to their teaching and students.

Teachers must find a balance between this dichotomy. Teachers should be willing to place themselves in dissonance in order for their students to also go there. Teachers need to model civil discourse and difficult dialogues so that students learn how to do so in other life spaces.

It is healthy for teachers to approach difficult topics such as racism and death and admit that they don't have all the answers. Death and loss is a topic everyone will encounter in their lifetime. And as long as communities of people continue to be brutalized by injustices, either natural or humanmade, schools and communities will have lessons to learn and teach. Teachers can only hope to impact the world and make the world less brutal by learning lessons from the mistakes humanity seems destined to make.

BOX 9.1 CONNECTED RESOURCES

Dartmouth. (2011, April 11). *TEDxDartmouth 2011—Michael Chaney: How to read a graphic novel* [Video file]. Retrieved from https://www.youtube.com/watch?v=qAyEbgSPi9w

Michael Chaney shares how graphic novels have evolved from comic books to complex, socially situated texts.

Nothum, S. (2014). *A simple, informal intro to graphic novels* [Video file]. Retrieved from https://www.youtube.com/watch?v=wHVyUOHVmnE

Nothum energetically introduces his class to graphic novels, giving a historical scaffold for their origination and current forms.

McCloud, S. (1994). *Understanding comics: The invisible art.* New York, NY: Harper Perrenial.

McCloud's groundbreaking text walks the reader through the various parts of the comic structure, emphasizing the balance of critical thinking and art that each artist uses in creating their work.

Spiegelman, A. (1996). *The complete Maus.* New York, NY: Pantheon Books.
Stassen. (2006). *Deogratis: A tale of Rwanda.* New York, NY: First Second Books.

Both *Maus* and *Deogratis* offer additional perspectives of brutalized communities in graphic form.

REFERENCES

The Art Story Foundation. (2017). Movements, styles and tendencies: Kinetic art. Retrieved from http://www.theartstory.org/movement-kinetic-art.htm
Beach, R., Appleman, D., Hynds, S., and Wilhelm, J. (2006). *Teaching literature to adolescents.* New York, NY: Routledge.
Brown, D. (2015). *Drowned city: Hurricane Katrina & New Orleans.* Boston, MA: Houghton Mifflin Harcourt.

Copeland, M. (2005). *Socratic circles: Fostering critical and creative thinking in middle and high school.* Portland, ME: Stenhouse Publishers.

McCloud, S. (1994). *Understanding comics: The invisible art.* New York, NY: Harper Perrenial.

National Council of Teachers of English and International Reading Association. (2012). *NCTE/IRA standards for the English language arts.* Retrieved from http://www.ncte.org/standards/ncte-ira

Wilhelm, J. (2016). *"You gotta be the book": Teaching engaged and reflective reading with adolescents.* New York, NY: Teachers College Press.

Part IV

WAR AND GENOCIDE

Chapter 10

Discussing War-Related Death and Trauma through Storytelling in *The Things They Carried*

Gretchen Rumohr-Voskuil and
Deborah Vriend Van Duinen

According to the 2014 U.S. Census Bureau, of 319.2 million Americans, there were 21.8 million veterans of the U.S. armed forces (Risen, 2014), making it likely that most students have friends or family members that have served active duty. Specific to Tim O'Brien's (2009) *The Things They Carried*, originally published in 1990, the 2015 U.S. Census Bureau (2016) reports that there are 6.8 million Vietnam veterans living in the United States, and still a quarter-million Vietnam War veterans suffering from post-traumatic stress disorder (Handwerk, 2015).

These statistics alone warrant the use of a Vietnam or war-related text in literature courses. In fact, many books that are part of the American high school curriculum are connected to death, but few force the reader to have direct discussions about it. This is not true for *The Things They Carried*. Considered a "classic" text in many high school classrooms, it was a finalist for the Pulitzer Prize and the National Book Critics Circle Award and is one of the titles included in the National Endowment for the Art's Big Read program.

Included in both high school and college literature canons, the book helps readers consider how individuals cope with death in personal ways, providing rich opportunities for discussion in communities affected by deployment in recent or not-so-recent years.

SUMMARY OF *THE THINGS THEY CARRIED*

The Things They Carried is part memoir and part fiction, based on O'Brien's experiences as an infantryman in the Vietnam War. However, it is not a typical combat story of glory and patriotism and does not contain the traditional narrative arc with a beginning, middle, and end. Instead, it is a text that travels between present and past, delving in brutal and sometimes humorous ways into the complexities of war, death, truth, and memory.

The book consists of a series of twenty-two interconnected vignettes that describe a fictional company of American soldiers fighting in Vietnam in 1969. This platoon of infantrymen includes Lieutenant Jimmy Cross, Kiowa, Dave Jensen, Curt Lemon, Ted Lavender, Norman Bowker, and Tim O'Brien. They get hit by sniper fire, laugh at each other's stories, walk through harsh conditions, and sit in silence as they try to make sense of it.

Some of the vignettes take place "in the moment," whereas others occur twenty years later. In the final chapter, *The Lives of the Dead*, O'Brien remembers his very first encounter with a dead body. His childhood crush, Linda, died at the age of nine from a brain tumor and O'Brien is deeply impacted by her death. He reflects on how soldiers in Vietnam kept the dead alive by telling stories about them and how, in this way, he keeps Linda alive by telling her story.

STORYTELLING AS AN APPROACH FOR TEACHING *THE THINGS THEY CARRIED*

The Things They Carried, in its entirety or in excerpts, serves as a springboard text to discuss the complexities of the Vietnam War, and war in general, with its honest and at times graphic portrayals of death, trauma, and grief. However, the book's larger questions about truth, memory, loss, and grief also compel readers to connect to the stories—and process their own experiences—even if they do not have war connections or traumas.

In an NPR interview in 2004, O'Brien acknowledged that young readers "bring such fervor to [reading the book] that comes from their own lives, really. The book is . . . applied to a bad childhood or a broken home. And these are the things they're carrying" (Conan, 2004). In the text, O'Brien (2009) explores the difference between happening-truth, the truth of fact or occurrence, and story-truth, the truth of fiction and emotional truth, making the reader question whether "telling the truth"—what O'Brien would label as "truth of fact"—is necessary in telling a true story.

In the chapter "Spin," O'Brien (2009) reflects,

> Forty-three years old, and the war occurred half a lifetime ago, and yet the remembering makes it now. And sometimes remembering will lead to a story, which makes it forever. That's what stories are for. Stories are for joining the past to the future. Stories are for those late hours in the night when you can't remember how you got from where you were to where you are. Stories are for eternity, when memory is erased, when there is nothing to remember except the story. (p. 36)

Throughout the book, O'Brien (2009) argues that storytelling or retelling helps people remember those who have been lost, allowing survivors to grapple with and try to make sense of these experiences.

O'Brien's belief in the power of story is supported by others. In *Story Proof: The Science behind the Startling Power of Story*, Kendall F. Haven (2007) writes, "The brain converts raw experience into story form and then considers, ponders, remembers, and acts on the self-created story, not the actual input experienced" (p. 29). This chapter acknowledges the value of stories in *The Things They Carried* as well as in students' personal lives as a way to process and communicate difficult life events and in that effort, the next sections detail pre, during, and postreading strategies through this lens of loss.

Prereading: Contextualizing the Vietnam War

Before reading *The Things They Carried*, teachers can provide background information on the Vietnam War, giving students information and context to understand the book's plot, themes, and relevance to American history, but not so much that it overshadows personal engagement with the text. This might include the information that Vietnam War veterans still suffer from post-traumatic stress disorder and other repercussions of combat trauma. Other helpful statistics can contextualize these conversations, especially the 58,220 U.S. casualties in the Vietnam War and the 1,611 soldiers still unaccounted for (CNN Library, 2017).

Additional resources on the Vietnam War provide background and context. Students can read excerpts from nonfiction texts such as Elizabeth Partridge's (2018) *Boots on the Ground: America's War in Vietnam*, which offers striking perspectives, events, and images.

Showing clips from the Ken Burns and Lynn Novick's (2017) ten-part, eighteen-hour documentary series, *The Vietnam War*, or the HBO documentary *Dear America: Letters Home from Vietnam* (2006), featuring letters from American soldiers in the Vietnam War, can help students better understand soldiers' experiences. Written in haikus, Chris Crowe's *Death Coming up the Hill* (2014) can provide additional context.

In addition, Texas Tech's (2013) Vietnam Center and Archive and the National Veterans Art Museum's website (2018) contain helpful teaching resources. When exploring these materials, teachers can utilize Kylene Beers and Bob Probst's (2015) close-reading techniques as they encourage students to point out contrasts or contradictions as well as absolute and extreme language. Providing historical context for students' reading of the text can enhance their understanding and allow them to personally connect to the book.

To introduce the stories that O'Brien carries and tells, teachers can ask students to draw a backpack and, using the backpack as a metaphor for life, list the things that weigh them down. Students should consider ways they, or others, could lighten their burdens. An autobiographical writing prompt (Wilhelm, 2007) can also be assigned to help readers front-load and connect personally with the text (see box 10.1).

BOX 10.1   AUTOBIOGRAPHICAL WRITING PROMPT: STORYTELLING AND SECRETS

Directions: Please respond to one of the following prompts as specifically as you can. At times, we may share a few of our ideas with one another in small groups, or revisit what you've written. You *will not* have to share the actual composition with anyone but me.

Choose one of the following options. As you write, please remember to concentrate on experiences you have actually had. Discuss in detail what happened, how you felt during and after the experience, how the experience influenced your life, and so on.

A. Describe a time when you wanted something to happen a certain way, but it didn't. Maybe you wanted someone to like you, but they chose not to. Maybe someone got sick and you wanted him or her to be healthy again, but he or she died. Maybe you made a choice that you regretted. What happened? Why did you desire things to be different? Did you ever fantasize about a different outcome? What made this situation so hard? How did you deal with it? Do you still feel sad/guilty/angry today? Why or why not?

B. Describe a time that you kept something important completely to yourself—a time that you kept a secret. Perhaps you did something you didn't want anyone to know about. Perhaps you made a decision on your own and didn't want to let anyone else in on the process. Regardless of your secret, you do not need to tell me what the secret is. Just think about the time that you kept the secret. Is it still a secret? Why did you keep it a secret? What did you do in order to maintain secrecy? If you did eventually tell, why did you choose to tell, and how did you feel afterward? Did you ever fantasize about telling your secret someone? How has keeping a secret influenced you as a person?

C. Describe a time when you lost someone or something important to you, for good. If you feel comfortable writing about it, who/what was it, and what make this so important to you? How was it lost? How did you feel, and how did you react, considering this loss? Did you ever fantasize about a different outcome? How do you feel about this loss (and writing about it) today?

Teachers could also respond to these prompts along with the students. Regarding the topic of death and grieving, Ungemah (2017) affirms this critical witnessing: "Just as we ask students to be their true selves in the classroom—to be honest, open, and vulnerable—as a pedagogical imperative, we must do the same" (p. 54).

Having students consider the ways that minds form, process, experience, and perhaps even revise various experiences—as each prompt encourages them to do via their consideration of different outcomes—can, in turn, encourage them to weigh how their "truths" align with O'Brien's (2009) "truths" (i.e., happening-truth, story-truth, and others) employed in his stories.

For example, the account of killing a man considers several different people at fault, showing the reader how O'Brien (2009) uses storytelling to process this event from different angles. Students consider different outcomes in their own stories, and how such fantasizing helped or hindered their ability to make sense of what happened. They could also analyze how O'Brien's (2009) multiple perspective strategy helps him process these experiences in healthy ways and in turn explore how to use this strategy for themselves.

O'Brien (2009) uses storytelling as a way to resurrect those he has lost. He tells his stories, to others but perhaps most importantly to himself, as a way of saving his own soul, of trying to make sense with who he now is and who he wants to be.

In similar ways, students have or will encounter traumatic events in their lives just as O'Brien encountered trauma in his life. As they write, prompt students to think about how they felt and how they remember this person. By mirroring O'Brien's (2009) control over his stories, students can remember that though they may not have had control over the events in their lives, they do have control over how they write about such events and outcomes.

During Reading: Truth and Tableaus

This section highlights some of the chapters that address death, loss, and dying. Other chapters from the book can be used, but the ones given next model various modes of response. A brief summary of each story is provided first, followed by activities and discussion questions.

"On Rainy River"

In this story, O'Brien learns that he is drafted to the Vietnam War and considers running away to Canada. He finds refuge with an older man by the border who gives him a chance to escape. In the end, O'Brien decides not to dodge the draft after considering how his family, reputation, and future plans will be negatively affected by running away. Ironically, O'Brien concludes that his reasons for returning to fight were neither noble nor brave.

"How to Tell a True War Story"

In this story, O'Brien explores what it means to tell a "true" war story by using examples of tales from his fellow soldiers. He concludes that the truth of a story is not as important as what the story is trying to say.

"The Man I Killed"

As the title suggests, this story accounts for a man killed by O'Brien as well as the manner in which he killed him. O'Brien imagines what the man was like prior to the war and in doing so, reminds readers that the stories people tell do not always have happy endings, and can bring more feelings of guilt than absolution.

"Ambush"

When O'Brien's daughter asks if he killed anyone in the war, he tells her that he did not. He then launches into a story of an ambush led by his platoon that led to the killing of a young man who may or may not have been ready to fight.

"In the Field"

In this chapter, a member of the platoon, Kiowa, dies on the banks of a river. The other members of the platoon respond in different ways to his death—guilt, humor, and responsibility. At the end of the story, Kiowa's body is recovered from the mud.

Teachers can encourage students to visualize the text using Wilhelm's (2016) tableau strategy, focusing especially on moments when O'Brien's vivid storytelling seems to serve as a way to process loss. Tableau activities require that students read the text carefully, block the scene according to the text and their own artistic license, and consider O'Brien's motivations and decisions in writing the story this particular way.

Tableaus can also help teachers check for reading comprehension, and taking photos of each tableau allows students to revisit and compare these scenes with others throughout their reading of the text. Focusing on loss, possible tableau assignments include the moment of decision on the Rainy River (pp. 54–57), O'Brien's (2009) attempted account of Curt Lemon's death (pp. 66–68), Tim's inability to move after seeing a dead man (pp. 123–24), the revision of Tim's killing story (pp. 126–27), and the search for Kiowa (pp. 155–57).

There are multiple opportunities to further consider how storytelling impacts O'Brien's (2009) exploration of death and loss, and well-planned discussion questions can aid in this discovery. Some general questions about storytelling are included in table 10.1 along with Brian White's (1993) "authentic questions," which fall into three categories: prediction, author's generalization, and structural generalization.

While discussing textual matters, students can offer their opinions in low-risk ways, and then ask how the text supports these assertions. Hollie's (2015) "my two cents" strategy encourages equitable participation, asking students to place a penny on the table the first time they participate, and then wait to respond again after other group members have placed their coin.

Discussion questions also serve as journal quick-writes, beginning-of-class prompts, or exit slips, allowing students to communicate struggles or victories with textual comprehension and engagement. In these instances, such questions encourage students to read texts closely, considering theme, characterization, craft, and structure.

Postreading: Connecting Our Stories with Others'

Students may desire to process the novel by learning from veterans in their own communities. Teachers can utilize personal or familial connections or reach out to their local veterans' chapters and ask veterans to share their war-related stories in their classrooms. Inviting local veterans allows for further consideration on themes of loss and storytelling as teachers can ask them to respond to particular chapters in light of their own wartime experiences. Focusing on the text can help veterans know what to talk about, giving them the space to share similar or different experiences and viewpoints.

Revisiting their autobiographical writings, students can respond, aligning or differing from O'Brien's (2009) perspective. Ideas include the following statements: "Sometimes remembering will lead to a story, which makes it forever. That's what stories are for. Stories are for joining the past to the future" (p. 36); "What stories can do, I guess, is make things present. I can look at things I never looked at. I can attach faces to grief and love and pity and God. I can be brave. I can make myself feel again" (pp. 171–72); and "Stories can save us . . . in a story, which is a kind of dreaming, the dead sometimes smile and sit up and return to the world" (p. 212).

Considering their work with stories and veterans up to this point, students can explore in concrete ways how storytelling construction communicates truth by writing original autobiographies about loss or revisiting their auto-biographical writing prompts, revising for details, language, and structure.

Channeling the power of Tom Romano's (2000) multigenre projects, students can rewrite their stories into other genres. Ideas include merging

Table 10.1.   Questions to Guide Students' Reading of *The Things They Carried*

General Questions for Each Chapter	White's (1993) "Authentic Questions"
What do you notice about how O'Brien describes death or loss?	*Prediction:*
How does this representation align with how you represented death/loss in your autobiographical writing?	1. (After O'Brien's decision to "submit" to war, p. 58) What do you suppose are some of the most important things that O'Brien will lose as a result of his decision? Gain?
In your opinion, what is O'Brien trying to accomplish personally and as a writer by telling the story this way?	2. (After O'Brien describes the man he supposedly killed, p. 123) Do you think Kiowa and Tim will remember this killing as it actually happened? Why or why not?
What do you think was given up in telling the story this way? What do you think was lost?	3. (As Cross considers writing a letter, p. 170) If Cross wrote a letter, what do you think it might say?
What are some of the inferences and literary devices that you notice in the story?	*Author's Generalization:*
What details are included in the story? What are excluded? Is the story contradictory?	1. (Discussing Tim's decision regarding whether he should flee the war, p. 48) What do you suppose O'Brien is trying to say about grief/about loss/about decision making through the description of his time at the cabin?
In your opinion, who benefits from the telling of the story? Do others benefit?	2. (At the conclusion of "How to Tell a True War Story") What do you suppose O'Brien is trying to say about truth with his various accounts of Curt Lemon's death?
How do you see the story as "true" and how does it align with what O'Brien says about story-truth? (p. 171).	3. (At the conclusion of "In the Field") What do you suppose O'Brien is trying to say about blame through the story of Lieutenant Cross? The young soldier?
	Structural Generalization:
	1. (Throughout the book, but especially between "The Man I Killed" and "Ambush") How do you think this story would be different, especially regarding Tim's guilt, if we'd read the "happening truth" before the "story truth"?
	2. (After "Ambush") In your opinion, how might this book have been different without the chapter "On the Rainy River"?
	3. (At conclusion of the book) In your opinion, how might this book have been different if O'Brien had changed the "story truth" to include more significant injuries to himself (e.g., loss of a limb)?

narratives with "found" poems that utilize lines from the novel or nonfiction Vietnam War resources; creating obituaries and other memorials; compiling images and explanations of loss from their own lives or the lives of others; telling their stories of loss with episodic fiction or six-word memoirs; curating a multigenre, loss-focused collection. Experimenting with form and offering student choice communicates to students that there is power in telling stories of loss on their own terms.

Audio stories, such as the ones found on Storycorp.org, can provide access to other story construction and veteran experience. With goals that mirror Romano's (2000) multigenre project, students could interview veterans, classmates, family, or community members about stories of loss and construct and revise them as per StoryCorp guidelines. These accounts can be posted to StoryCorp's website or compiled and shared with the immediate community as a testament to the power of stories.

CAUTIONS AND ADVICE

Discussions with students about wartime and other deaths can pose unique challenges. As O'Brien's text suggests, remembering and reflecting on death can be messy, contradictory, surprising, and difficult; yet, this is why this text is so important. *The Things They Carried* does not promise its readers an easy walk through a difficult subject, and yet it does provide solace and even hope to its readers. Stories can save people.

Value of stories aside, it should be noted that some school districts have resisted the book due to its use of profanity and graphic content. Also, politics surrounding war and the ways that patriotism might or should be expressed in war are topics that can lead to division in the classroom. Additionally, students' personal experiences with post-traumatic stress disorder should be considered prior to reading the book.

While the aforementioned concerns are real, they are not reasons to avoid using the book. Instead, such concerns highlight the need to build trust with students, colleagues, parents, and administrators; plan instruction carefully, scaffolding for potentially troubling content; and through journaling and other responses, enable students to communicate when they are struggling to process difficult stories or concepts.

Each of these strategies empower teachers and students to read *The Things They Carried* and other books that "do not lie to the young about the perilous but wondrous times we live in, [but rather] books which talk of the fears, hopes, joys, and frustrations people experience, books about people not only as they are but as they can be" (National Council of Teachers of English, 2009, para. 17).

CONCLUSION

Processing death and loss through storytelling and retelling is affirmed by Brittany Rose Collins (2017), who asserts in "Associative Mourning: Learning to Lose through Literature" that the study of death through literature provides a "'safe' and alternate vehicle for affective and intellectual reactions to loss, shaping the schemata through which students view their self-created stories" (p. 48). In other words, books such as *The Things They Carried* open new doors and opportunities and provide structure as students process their own experiences with death.

Reflecting on O'Brien's affective and intellectual reactions to loss in the pages of *The Things They Carried* as well as their own stories about death, loss, and grief allows students exactly that. However, it also does more. O'Brien's use of storytelling to remember and reflect on those who have died—and loss as a whole—offers direction, empowerment, and ultimately, hope.

BOX 10.2   CONNECTED RESOURCES

Myers, W. D. (2008, 2009). *Fallen angels* and *Sunrise over Fallujah*. New York, NY: Scholastic.

Myers has crafted companion stories of an African American unit in Vietnam and an Iraq war story of a group of enlistees, helping readers to contextualize and diversify combat-related issues.

Crowe, C. (2014). *Death coming up the hill*. Boston, MA: HMH books for young readers.

This story, told from the perspective of a seventeen years old American boy in 1968 in haiku poems, explores the ways that combat affects the lives of veterans as well as families. Crowe's collection can augment the teaching of O'Brien through its content and form.

Anderson, L. H. (2014). *The impossible knife of memory*. New York, NY: Viking Books for Young Readers.

Anderson's book paints a realistic, yet tender, picture of the aftermath of Iraq combat, weaving relevantly with O'Brien's depictions of postwar life.

Doller, T. (2012). *Something like normal*. New York, NY: Bloomsbury USA Children's.

This story explores the value of getting professional help after traumatic events, contrasting with the way that O'Brien fails to mention similar postcombat support.

Boianjiu, S. (2013). *The people of forever are not afraid*. New York, NY: Hogarth.

Told in a multilayered, multistory fashion not unlike O'Brien's prose, Boianjiu's book focuses on Israeli teenage girls who join the army, allowing for discussions about gender and death.

Percy, B., Ponsoldt, J., & Novgorodoff, D. (2009). *Refresh, refresh: A graphic novel*. New York, NY: First Second.

This graphic novel profiles a group of boys whose fathers are all serving in Iraq and allows visual learners to connect more fully with combat issues.

REFERENCES

Beers, G. K., & Probst, R. E. (2015). *Reading nonfiction: Notice & note stances, signposts, and strategies.* Portsmouth, NH: Heinemann.

Burns, K., & Novick, L. (Directors and Producers). (2017). *The Vietnam War* [DVD]. Arlington: PBS.

CNN Library. (2017, March 27). *Vietnam War fast facts.* Retrieved from http://www.cnn.com/2013/07/01/world/vietnam-war-fast-facts/index.html

Conan, N. (Host). (2010, March 24). "The Things They Carried," 20 years on [Radio broadcast episode]. Retrieved from https://www.npr.org/templates/story/story.php?storyId=125128156

Couturie, B. (Director). (2006). *Dear America: Letters home from Vietnam* [DVD], In B. Couturié, T. Bird & B. Edelman (Producers). New York City: HBO.

Handwerk, B. (2015). Over a quarter-million Vietnam veterans still have PTSD. *Smithsonian Magazine.* Retrieved from https://www.smithsonianmag.com/science-nature/over-quarter-million-vietnam-war-veterans-still-have-ptsd-180955997/

Haven, K. F. (2007). *Story proof: The science behind the startling power of story.* Santa Barbara, CA: Libraries Unlimited.

Hollie, S. (2015). *Strategies for culturally and linguistically responsive teaching and learning.* Huntington Beach, CA: Shell Education.

National Council of Teachers of English. (2009). *The students' right to read.* Retrieved from http://www2.ncte.org/statement/righttoreadguideline/

National Veterans Art Museum. (2018). *National Veterans Art Museum.* Retrieved from http://www.nvam.org/

O'Brien, T. (2009). *The things they carried.* New York, NY: First Mariner Books.

Risen, T. (2014, November 10). Veterans Day data boot camp. *U.S. News and World Report.* Retrieved from https://www.usnews.com/news/blogs/data-mine/2014/11/10/veterans-day-data-boot-camp

Romano, T. (2000). *Blending genre, altering style: writing multigenre papers.* Portsmouth, NH: Boynton Cook Publishers.

Ungemah, L. (2017). The absolutely true diary of my accidental (and successful) unit studying death. *English Journal, 107*(2), 53–58.

U.S. Census Bureau. (2016, October 25). *Newsroom: Facts for features Veterans Day 2016: Nov. 11.* Retrieved from https://www.census.gov/newsroom/facts-for-features/2016/cb16-ff21.html

Texas Tech University (2013). *The Vietnam Center and Archive.* Retrieved from https://www.vietnam.ttu.edu/

White, B. (1993). Pulling students toward meaning or making meaning with students: Asking authentic questions in the literature classroom. *Language Arts Journal of Michigan, 9*(1), 28–40.

Wilhelm, J. (2007). *Engaging readers and writers with inquiry.* New York, NY: Scholastic.

Wilhelm, J. (2016). *You gotta BE the book: Teaching engaged and reflective reading with adolescents.* New York, NY: Teachers College Press.

Chapter 11

Discussing War and Death with *A Separate Peace* by John Knowles

Leilya Pitre and Steven T. Bickmore

One of the first experts on teaching young adult literature Robert Carlsen (1984) once noted that "books had a life expectancy of twenty to thirty years" (p. 30). Published in 1959, nearly a decade before the commonly acknowledged birth of the adolescent novel in 1967, *A Separate Peace* by John Knowles (2003) has far outlived that life expectancy prediction.

Twenty years after its first publication, it was on the list of English teachers' favorite novels (Judy & Judy, 1979) and is still popular in the high school English classroom with readily available teacher guides aligned with the federal, state, and NCTE/IRA Content Standards in English for grades ninth to twelfth.

Like *The Catcher in the Rye* (Salinger, 1951), *The Lord of the Flies* (Golding, 1954), and *The Bell Jar* (Plath, 1963), *A Separate Peace* is a novel not written directly for adolescents, yet it encapsulates many of the issues: loss of innocence, bullying, suicide, war, and death that have come to be hallmarks of the adolescent realistic problem novel.

Told from the main character, Gene Forrester's adolescent point of view, the novel has become a constant reminder in high school classrooms that even though a war may rage overseas (World War II, Viet Nam, Gulf War, and the Iraq) and hover over students in the classroom, death can visit unexpectedly and often violently near to home. The constant teaching of this novel can and should be a reminder that adolescents deal with trauma, death, and grief more frequently that we often imagine or acknowledge.

SUMMARY OF *A SEPARATE PEACE*

To face his fears, Gene Forrester, the narrator of *A Separate Peace*, takes readers through a retrospective journey of his 1942–1943 school year.

Framed as an extended flashback, Gene is revisiting his alma mater, Devon, fifteen years after graduation to face "fearful sights" from that tumultuous year. The school and its students exist under the shadow of World War II and its increasing intensity as event after event reminds them that war is reaching out to include them in its ominous embrace.

The reader accompanies Gene as he visits two locations: first, a tree with its long thin limb extending out over the river, and second, a white marble flight of stairs. From the beginning of the flashback, the setting creates an idyllic tone that is slowly undercut. However, the true focus of impending doom is located in relationships. It is primarily the relationship between Gene and Phineas, or Finny, their friendship, innocence, and death as Gene attempts to reconcile his emotions and grief from Finny's unexpected and inconceivable death at the end of the school year.

WAR AT THE HOME FRONT: FROM HOME TO WAR AND BACK AGAIN

This novel is more than about Finny's individual death. Moreover, it is about death during war that affects friendship, the homefront, and a loss of innocence. World War II is oppressively present throughout the novel, and as Gene notices, "The war would be deadly all right" (pp. 100–101) because at that time, there simply could not be a "question about it [death] at all; it was there" (Knowles, 2003, p. 101). Bringing this novel into the classroom means engaging in sensitive and painful issues, especially if the issue is an integral part of the discussion.

What is the best way to begin a conversation about death and loss of the loved ones? How can teachers prepare high school students to discuss these matters and help them cope with the loss? To answer these questions, Leilya developed several activities for teaching *A Separate Peace*. She decided to let her preservice English teachers in a college course on young adult literature explore these activities and evaluate their effectiveness.

Building Background for Thoughtful Exploration

Practice shows that it is helpful to start with building background knowledge. Strong prereading activities will prepare students to tackle complicated tasks and meaningful discussions. To build background knowledge before reading the novel, Leilya assigned a student, Adam D., to be an expert on the novel and its author. Adam introduced John Knowles and the setting of the novel. He also presented facts regarding losses of human lives for each of the major allies in the war (See Dean, 2017 for statistical data).

Adam broke down the details of the World War II consequences, in terms of lives lost, for the participating nations, to demonstrate its global effect on the world. Leilya engaged these preservice teachers in a *Walk Down Memory Lane* activity, in which students journaled about any encounters they had with the war, whether directly or indirectly. Mostly these included brief narratives about their relatives, friends, or others who told stories of war or suffered its consequences.

Hurt by memories and reality, Jenna shared her father's story, a Vietnam War veteran, who still suffers post-traumatic stress disorder (PTSD) and attends weekly classes "to learn coping mechanisms." Savannah's story about her grandfather's friend was more tragic. After going into battle and seeing friends die, Jack, her grandfather's best friend, jumped off the railing of the ship into the open sea with the words "I cannot sleep at night with the things I've seen and done." That episode still haunts Savannah's grandfather.

Yet, another story told about Michelle's son-in-law, a former marine serving in Iraq and Afghanistan, who lost two friends in Fallujah, Iraq, and was severely injured while on patrol duty. Eight years later, with a Purple Heart and shrapnel in his chest, he still suffers from PTSD and often screams at night. These journal entries were heartbreaking, but they helped everyone realize the destructive nature of war for the mind and body of those affected by it.

Walk Down Memory Lane is an activity in which the preservice teachers shared their vulnerability and pain about the past experiences while learning how to teach and model these kinds of stories with their future students. Completing the activity, they realized how vital it is to be delicate and cautious when asking students to share and discuss very sensitive memories. It became an additional reminder of the importance of learning as much about one's students as possible before approaching subjects of war and death.

For secondary school students, *Walk Down Memory Lane* is an activity that allows students to learn about their own family history and, in some cases, family grief. Students may interview their grandparents, parents, and older relatives or neighbors to find out how the war—World War II, Vietnam, or Iraq Wars—has affected their loved ones. The results of this research activity may be presented in a form of a letter, a journal entry, or a drawing describing the event. Under careful orchestration, this activity may turn into a school-wide multigenre project creating an opportunity to share with other classes, parents, and community.

To further the conversation, this activity may grow into the discussion about *memory keepers* in the family. Who are they and why? Usually, these are the family elders—great-grandparents, grandparents, and, then gradually, parents. Teachers may suggest students to become a memory keeper in their family by recording personal important events in a diary or journal.

To begin this practice, teachers may offer a journal entry, for example: "Has anyone in your family experienced the loss of loved one? Or how do you think families can or do deal with the loss of loved ones. If possible, please, write about that time in your journal and explain your feelings." Another way to be memory keepers is to record stories told by the family elders detailing their feelings while grieving and noting what helped them heal.

Recording and sharing these stories might become important for students who are in communities that are removed from big tragedies—shootings, natural disasters, and so on—so that they can begin to think about how and what others might be experiencing.

Noting the Difficult: Finding Passages That Encourage Discussion

Without a doubt the best way to promote reading and meaningful discussion is actual reading. During reading *A Separate Peace*, it would be logical to spend some time on close reading of several excerpts dealing with death. This activity leads to *Lightning Round* immediate reaction/response to the passage, with no more than thirty seconds to respond, reflect, comment, or ask a question about the excerpt.

This activity can be completed as a whole group if there is a relatively small class of students, no more than twenty. A teacher may prepare excerpts for the whole-class activity (see box 11.1). If the class is bigger, it is more effective and engaging to complete it in groups of four or five. In this case, students may be assigned to choose up to three short, one- to two-paragraph excerpts from the given chapters for homework.

This is how it works. There are sixteen students in Leilya's class; this makes four groups of four students. In each group, one student reads an excerpt, and a student next to him or her responds with a comment, reaction, or question within thirty seconds. Then, this responding student reads his or her excerpt, and another student responds. This happens until all four students in a group have read and responded to an excerpt. If excerpts repeat, the response is still necessary because students may think and react to the same piece of reading differently.

Next is an example of one of the groups during *Lightning Round* activity. The first student, Brianna, reads an excerpt:

> Looking back now across fifteen years, I could see with great clarity the fear I had lived in, which must mean that in the interval I had succeeded in a very important undertaking: I have made my escape from it. I felt fear's echo, and along with that I felt the unhinged, uncontrollable joy which had been its accompaniment and opposite face, joy which had broken out sometimes in those days like Northern Lights across black sky. (Knowles, 2003, p. 10)

BOX 11.1   SUGGESTED PASSAGES FROM
A SEPARATE PEACE FOR A *LIGHTNING ROUND*
ACTIVITY

- "Looking back now across fifteen years, I could see with great clarity the fear I had lived in, which must mean that in the interval I had succeeded in a very important undertaking: I have made my escape from it. I felt fear's echo, and along with that I felt the unhinged, uncontrollable joy which had been its accompaniment and opposite face, joy which had broken out sometimes in those days like Northern Lights across black sky" (Knowles, 2003, p. 10).
- "The war would be deadly all right. But I was used to finding something deadly in things that attracted me; there was always something deadly lurking in anything I wanted, anything I loved. And if it wasn't there, as for example with Phineas, then I put it there myself" (Knowles, 2003, pp. 100–101).
- "Why go through the motions of getting an education and watch the war slowly chip away at the one thing I had loved here, the peace, the measureless, careless peace of the Devon summer? Others, the Quackenbushes of this world, could calmly watch the war approach them and jump into it at the last and most advantageous instant, as though buying into the stock market. But I couldn't" (Knowles, 2003, pp. 101).
- "But Phineas had moved in a continuous flowing balance, so that he had seemed to drift along with no effort at all, relaxation on the move. He hobbled now among the patches of ice. There was one certainty that Dr. Stanpole had given—Phineas would walk again. But the thought was there before me that he would never walk like that again" (Knowles, 2003, p. 111).
- "I want to fix your leg up," I said crazily but in a perfectly natural tone of voice which made my words sound even crazier, even to me. "You'll fix my . . ." and he arched out, lunging hopelessly into the space between us. He arched out and then fell, his legs still on the bed, his hands falling with a loud slap against the floor. Then after a pause all the tension drained out of him, and he let his head come slowly down between his hands. He had not hurt himself. But he brought his head slowly down between his hands and rested it against the floor, not moving, not making any sound. "I am sorry," I said blindly, "I'm sorry, I'm sorry" (Knowles, 2003, p. 185).
- "This is something I think boys of your generation are going to see a lot of," he said quietly, "and I will have to tell you about it now. Your friend is dead." He was incomprehensible. I felt an extremely cold chill along my back and neck, that was all. Dr. Stanpole went on talking incomprehensibly. "It was such a simple, clean break. Anyone could have set it. Of course, I didn't send him to Boston. Why should I?" (Knowles, 2003, p. 193).
- "I did not cry then or ever about Finny. I did not cry even when I stood watching him being lowered into his family's strait-laced burial ground outside of Boston. I could not escape a feeling that this was my own funeral, and you do not cry in that case" (Knowles, 2003, p. 194).
- "I never talked about Phineas and neither did anyone else; he was, however, present in every moment of every day since Dr. Stanpole had told me. Finny had a vitality which could not be quenched so suddenly, even by the marrow of his bone. That was why I couldn't say anything or listen to anything about him, because he endured so forcefully that what I had to say would have seemed crazy to anyone else—I could not use the past tense, for instance—and what they had to say would be incomprehensible to me. During the time I was with him, Phineas created an atmosphere in which I continued now to live, a way of sizing up the world with erratic and entirely personal reservations, letting its rocklike facts sift through and be accepted only a little at a time, only as much as he could assimilate without a sense of chaos and loss" (Knowles, 2003, p. 202).
- "All others at some point found something in themselves pitted violently against something in the world around them. With those of my year this point often came when they grasped the fact of the war. When they began to feel that there was this overwhelmingly hostile thing in the world with them, then the simplicity and unity of their characters broke and they were not the same again. Phineas alone had escaped this. He possessed an extra vigor, a heightened confidence in himself, a serene capacity for affection which saved him. Nothing as he was growing up at home, nothing at Devon, nothing even about the war had broken his harmonious and natural unity. So at last I had" (Knowles, 2003, p. 202–3).
- "I never killed anybody and I never developed an intense level of hatred for the enemy. Because my war ended before I ever put on a uniform; I was on active duty all my time at school; I killed my enemy there" (Knowles, 2003, p. 204).

Taylor, sitting next to Brianna, responds: "I guess Gene is trying to say that fear disappears when you don't face things scaring you. Like out of sight, out of mind." Amanda jumps in, "Can I say? No, I think he finally is free from fear after facing it for so many years after things happened," and Rachel supports: "Right. I also think that now he is free from that fear and full of joy." "I thought the joy was in connection with good memories of school days," Brianna explains her understanding of the quote she read.

While the instructions for a *Lightning Round* activity require one immediate response to one quote, this group demonstrates a mini-discussion of it, while the teacher doesn't interrupt. Walking around she hears the same kind of discussions at each table, and this is encouraging; students are thinking and trying to understand what each quote means to them or what it meant for the narrator.

After all groups complete their *Lightning Round* activity, the teacher brings class together to summarize small group discussions, note which excerpts are chosen, and further discuss the students' reactions and responses. Preservice teachers enjoyed the activity that gave them "a chance to really look closer at some parts of the novel and try to interpret it the way we understand," summarizes Adam.

This activity may be concluded with asking students to write a one- to two-paragraph response discussing the excerpt that seemed the most important to them, why it was vital to the development of the character, theme, or plot, or how it promoted their understanding of the novel. Writing would help students record one or two important thoughts they heard or expressed through the discussion.

Writing to Heal and Reflect

Writing as healing practice is a powerful tool (Haddix, 2017). It helps students relive and relieve their tensions and struggles. Moreover, connecting with literary characters, who went through the loss of the loved ones, enables students to recognize the universality of the experience: they are not alone. This understanding of belonging to a group of people with similar experiences is crucial; however, painful, unbearable, and heartbreaking it may seem.

Two writing activities that Leilya's students explore as enriching postreading mini-projects are a *War Journal* and a *Letter from the War*. While the assignment is similar, students have a choice to write in a format that they prefer.

The task expects students to imagine that they are the soldiers or are anticipating being soldiers during the war. In a letter or journal entry, they have to describe their experiences:

- What do you do and what do you see daily?
- How does this experience make you feel and affect your thinking and decision making?
- You may take a role of one of the novel characters—Leper, Brinker, Gene, or Phineas—imagining how they might have experienced the war.

In these journals and letters, students attempt to convey their understanding of war and the actions of the novel's characters in connection with it. One can almost "hear" desperation, pain, confusion, fear, and other feelings that Leper, Phineas, Brinker, Gene, and their classmates experienced in the novel through preservice teachers' writings. Their personal attitude toward war and death and change caused by the first two are inevitable results of thinking about the events in the novel.

Some of the students' thoughts are profoundly eye-opening and inspired not just from the novel reading, but from the building background knowledge and "Walk" activities that helped set the stage. For example, in a *Letter from War*, one "soldier" writes: "The people, the soldiers and men on the other side, are not all men. Some of these warriors are just *kids*. I try not to think about it." Understanding that German soldiers may not agree with their country's war mission, but must obey military orders, becomes blatantly profound.

In another letter, Savannah confesses how the war changes her and fellow soldiers:

We used to run in danger, eager to protect and fight for justice. We all used to write to our friends and family every chance we had. Now, it is so hard to find purpose or desire. I feel like I've lost myself in this war. We all did . . . We have changed and not for the better. We've all seen so much, heard so much, done so much. I want to erase it, but I can't.

Discussing this letter, students realize how war changes and affects people in ways they have not thought would be possible during peaceful time. The effect seems too destructive and painful.

Taking on a *War Journal* format, Blake writes:

We are getting closer to the front now. Sleeping at night, you can hear the faint bursts from the artillery fire in the distance. I always count how lucky I am to be here and not there with all those poor fellows. But today I saw something strange. In the mud, I saw a little ole flower. It was yellow with purple on the edges. Looking at it, I really saw a day a little brighter. Like it was a tiny sun keeping me and all these poor saps warm in this cold death march for freedom. Maybe our days will be counted a little longer because of it.

The author of this journal entry is hopeful that the war will end granting his friends and him some more time in this world. Sharing it with classmates, Blake brings in the idea that war can be merciful or hopeful at least, and some people will live to tell stories about it.

Presented are just a few examples of the activities that will work in a high school classroom and result in rich, meaningful discussions allowing students to be engaged and learn. These activities taught the preservice teachers in Leilya's class how to begin a conversation about the loss of a loved one, how to carefully invite and include students in sharing their personal emotions in connection with the death, beginning with analyzing the novel's characters and their reactions to traumatic events.

Moreover, sharing with peers brought them closer as a group of students in the same learning environment, thus helping to build coping mechanisms for grief. Depending on the class makeup, students' number, their background knowledge, and learning preferences, the activities can be easily modified or adjusted to meet their needs.

CAUTIONS AND ADVICE

Teaching about death can be daunting, mostly because it does not result in any definite answers. The only definite reality is that life ends, and those who are left mourning have more questions than answers.

However, teachers should not shy away from the subject. Census data prove that one in twenty children will most likely lose a parent by the time he or she graduates from high school, not counting that some will also lose a sibling, close friend, or other relative (American Federation of Teachers & New York Life Foundation, 2012). Research by New York Life Foundation confirms that seven out of ten teachers have at least one student in their classroom who is grieving (American Federation of Teachers & New York Life Foundation, 2012, p. 2).

After reading the novel, one of the preservice English majors in a college young adult literature course shared that "it was painful to read. I cried, especially at the end of the novel." Another student expressed the similar sentiment connecting the reading to personal experience: "When I read about Finny's passing during the surgery, I remembered my grandfather. He also died during surgery, and we just couldn't believe it." These quotes continuously remind teachers that they need to know their students and struggles with which these students deal.

Despite emotional struggles and heartbreaking personal encounters with death, preservice teachers believe it is necessary to talk about it in the English classroom. However, novels like *A Separate Peace* may not be a great choice at the beginning of the school year. Knowing students and building trustworthy relationships, in addition to creating a safe classroom environment where discussions and different perspectives are welcomed, would enhance the learning experience. "Because of the pain and the confusion of losing a loved one," cautions Lou, "teachers must approach the topic with a heart of patience, love, and understanding."

The helpful advice given by one the preservice teachers, Blake, is "to let the novels and stories teach the most complicated and sensitive topics." He believed that "if we choose the right book, it can really take care of that for us." Teachers, then, are able to guide their students through the emotions and challenges they encounter while reading, thinking, and discussing these issues.

Another priceless learning opportunity for students is meeting a war veteran. Inviting a person who witnessed the horrors of the war is an incredibly valuable experience for students. There are still some World War II veterans with us, and even more veterans who participated in the wars in Vietnam, Iraq, or Afghanistan. Besides personal connections, veterans could be located through local Veterans of Foreign Wars posts. These veterans would be able to tell about their lived experiences and share about pain, destruction, and death any war brings.

CONCLUSION

Despite adults' innate desire to shield adolescents from pain, they deal with trauma, death, and grief more habitually than we admit. Consequently, one of the most common sentiments among the preservice teachers summarized and articulated by Kadra is that "death is a topic that cannot be avoided; it will affect everyone at some point in their life, so we might as well face it."

Moreover, a distinct privilege of teaching literature is that it "brings into the classroom universal themes, such as love, friendship, hatred, betrayal and loss," and it opens the opportunities for discussions, in which novels, stories, and characters "help our students getting through their personal pain without even realizing it," asserts Taylor.

Thinking about ways to approach sensitive issues of war, death, loss, and emotional healing in the classroom becomes an integral part of teacher's job. Carefully choosing and crafting activities may assist young adults recognize their personal struggles, face them, and find the paths in which reading, interaction with the text, writing, and discussions convert into pivotal points of rebirth and recovery.

BOX 11.2   CONNECTED RESOURCES

Coalition to Support Grieving Students. (2018). *Guidelines for responding to a death of a student or school staff.* Retrieved from https://moyerfoundation.org/resources/guidelines-for-responding-to-a-death-of-a-student-or-school-staff/

These guidelines are developed to provide initial help to administrators and school faculty in response to a loss that affected the school, for example, a death of a student, which impacted an entire school community, like in *A Separate Peace.*

Poland, S., & Poland, D. (2004, April). Dealing with death at school. *Principal Leadership, 4*(8), 8–12.

This article serves as a preparation guide for any teacher who may face the death of a member of the school community, providing teachable moments that lead students and faculty to healing after the loss.

Giff, P. R. (1997). *Lily's crossing.* New York: Delacorte.

Lily fights World War II at home. She suffers as her widow father joins the war effort as a soldier. She is forced to live with her Gram. Gram is demanding, her closest friends most relocate so her father can work in a factory, and her only option for friendship seems to be a young Hungarian refugee. Albert and Lily develop a friendship that allows them both to face their fears.

REFERENCES

American Federation of Teachers, & New York Life Foundation. (2012, December 10). *Grief in the classroom* [Data file]. Retrieved from https://www.aft.org/sites/default/files/release_bereavement121012.pdf

Carlsen, G. R. (1984). Teaching literature for the adolescent: A historical perspective. *English Journal, 73*(7), 28–30.

Dean, M. (2017, May 17). World War 2 casualties [Blog post]. Retrieved from http://www.worldwar2facts.org/world-war-2-casualties.html

Golding, W. (1954). *Lord of the flies*. New York, NY: The Berkley Publishing Group.

Haddix, M. (June, 2017). *Writing our lives as a space of healing in troubling times*. Keynote presented at the Conference on English Education, Columbus, OH.

Judy, S., & Judy, S. (1979). English teacher's literary favorites: The results of a survey. *English Journal, 68*(2), 6–9.

Knowles, J. (2003). *A separate peace*. New York, NY: Scribner.

Plath, S. (1963). *The bell jar*. New York, NY: Heinemann.

Salinger, J. D. (1951). *The catcher in the rye*. Boston: Little, Brown and Company.

Chapter 12

"We Were Dangerous, and Brainwashed to Kill": Death and Resilience in *A Long Way Gone: Memoirs of a Boy Soldier*

Janine Julianna Darragh and Ashley S. Boyd

Turning on the news or scrolling through social media, one is bombarded with horrific images of violence, war, and displaced people around the globe. While many secondary students in the United States most likely have some experience with loss, they are less likely to have experienced war and the widespread death, trauma, and destruction that come with it. How can teachers broach the topics of death and loss, on both individual and grand levels? Literature can be an effective vehicle for speaking about the unspeakable.

Not only does literature provide a common "story" by which to learn, explore, and vicariously experience life's joys and sorrows, but it also allows for thoughtful discussion and exploration of the topic of death specifically as it relates to war and can help students resist propagating stereotypes of how violent and terrible "others" are. This can thereby bring humans together in their global citizenship and encourage their responsibility for standing up for the vulnerable in our own country and beyond.

Seeking to explore the potential power of young adult literature, this chapter will share ideas for teaching Ishmael Beah's (2007) *A Long Way Gone: Memoirs of a Boy Soldier* in the high school classroom focusing on the themes of death in war, child soldiers, and global responsibility. In addressing those themes, teachers can help students to better understand both the world around them and their capacity to act in that world.

SUMMARY OF *A LONG WAY GONE: MEMOIRS OF A BOY SOLDIER*

In *A Long Way Gone: Memoirs of a Boy Soldier*, Ishmael Beah (2007) recounts his experiences and the ways in which he was "touched by war"

137

(p. 6) in his country of Sierra Leone. When the book begins, Ishmael, at the age of twelve, fled from the rebels who were attacking his village. By the time he was thirteen, and with limited choices, Beah joined the government army. There, he and numerous other children were trained to kill, kept largely in a drugged state, and tried to forget their past so they could survive the present and have a future.

After his lieutenant turns him over to UNICEF, Ishmael was taken to a rehabilitation center that worked on detoxing and deprogramming the young soldiers. With much time and constant reminders of "This isn't your fault, you know. It really isn't. You'll get through this" (Beah, 2007, p. 151), Ishmael slowly began to heal. Soon after, he was invited to tell his story to the United Nations in New York City, where he met a woman who would become his foster parent. She encouraged him to share his experiences with others to make them aware of and advocate for the rights of children, especially those who may be living in war-torn nations.

Often painfully horrific and graphic in detail, Beah's (2007) memoir seamlessly weaves together three parts of his experience: the events that led up to his becoming a child soldier, his "rehabilitation," and his eventual escape from violence. When he was twelve years old, Beah's village was attacked. Thus began Beah's journey wandering from village to village with his friends and brother, trying to find their families and to survive.

At the age of thirteen, Beah is conscripted as a soldier. He is taught how to use a gun and kill on command. He is brainwashed and drugged and constantly told, "Visualize the enemy, the rebels who killed your parents, your family, and those who are responsible for everything that has happened to you" (Beah, 2007, p. 112). With these thoughts in mind, Beah and his fellow child soldiers become killing machines, and would have remained so, if his lieutenant had not turned him over to UNICEF for rehabilitation.

The rehabilitation process is challenging, and the child soldiers have to overcome their addictions and learn how to cope with their losses, what they have seen, and what they have done. Beah's (2007) honest, harrowing descriptions offer the reader a firsthand account of how humans can find themselves in unspeakable situations. Despite these events, however, Ishmael also shows the great resilience of children—and the possibilities for healing and regaining hope—despite the most tragic of life experiences.

TEACHING APPROACHES

Further we offer suggestions for using this text as a vehicle to help students form or reconsider their opinions about death, specifically about death and war and death in conjunction with child soldiers. We conclude with suggestions to guide students in considering their global responsibility through the development of social action projects.

Helping Students (Re)Form Opinions about Death and War

While students may have experienced loss and death of loved ones—be it family members or friends—large-scale death on foreign soil due to war and conflict may be a harder topic to which to relate. Death on the home front generally involves one person. While the death may be unexpected, there are usually rituals, procedures, and steps that are taken. There are experts who can provide support, be they doctors and nurses in hospitals, religious leaders, people from the mortuary or a funeral home, counselors, neighbors, family, or friends. While the loss may be unbearable, there are often others to help support, guide, and lighten the burden.

In war settings, there are no rules. Death is often widespread, with multiple lives lost in an instant. There generally is not time to process death, nor are there the physical and emotional supports in place for individuals dealing with loss. Death in war is different from death on the home front. The chaos and lack of rules and procedures regarding death in a battle zone are hard to comprehend. In order to help make sense of such atrocities, people may start to emotionally distance themselves from the war setting.

In fact, seeing accounts of war on news and social media might promulgate "othering" stereotypes. Ideas about "those people" can be easily formed when sitting in the comfort of one's school or home. Individuals in wars abroad are often depicted as violent, uneducated, and savage. The histories and contexts of warring countries are often glossed over or are too dense to provide in media coverage and thus mold a superficial perspective of those involved.

In teaching books about death in war, it is imperative, then, to focus on the complexity of the situation and the humanity of the people involved. This is not something *they* are doing; rather, it is something that is being done to people, to human beings. In Beah's (2007) memoir, for example, graphic descriptions of savagery abound, but at his core, Ishmael is just a young boy who loves rap and Shakespeare, his friends, and his family.

In order to initiate critical thinking on the topic of war and death, teachers can lead a "Four Corners" (e.g., Teacher Toolkit, n.d.) or "Human Continuum" (e.g., Wormeli, 2005) activity where students listen to a series of statements and then physically move around the room (no talking!) to indicate where they "stand" on the issue. The four corners can be labeled as *strongly agree, agree, disagree, and strongly disagree*, or a spectrum of numbers can be assigned (i.e., one through ten) with one being *strongly agree* and ten being *strongly disagree*. Students determine a number for each statement to illustrate where their belief falls.

As an introduction to Beah's (2007) memoir and using these teaching tools, then, teachers might pose statements such as given here:

- Death in war is inevitable and justifiable.
- Death due to one's job is different from death outside of one's work (illness, natural causes, etc.)
- It is sometimes necessary to use children as soldiers in war, even if the result is the loss of young lives.

Teachers should consider stating these prompts verbally and providing them for students in writing. To begin, they can give students time to individually reflect and write a response with some ideas to support their stances. Teachers can then have students physically show where they stand on each issue, and let the discussion begin from there. Students might have personal experiences that warrant their opinions, or they might learn from the statements of their peers.

In listening and responding to their classmates' opinions, students are achieving English language arts standards for developing their speaking and listening skills. The intention of this activity is to serve as a catalyst for students to see how death in war might be different from death more commonly experienced and to explore viewpoints on those disparities. Starting the conversation here will allow for a foundation and reference point as students read and discuss death and war in the memoir.

For each statement, after students have identified their stance, teachers might extend this activity by having students think about whether or not their response would change if they looked at each statement through a different perspective. For example, teachers could ask: *How would the following respond to each of the same statements?*

- A leader of the country
- A mother of a soldier
- An eighteen-year-old on the verge of enlisting

Considering each of these points of view can help show students how war and death are nuanced and complicated issues. Responding to each also shows audience awareness and the capacity to adjust to a particular context. Humanizing the issue, especially through, for example, looking through the eyes of a mother, can facilitate students' better comprehension of how deeply war affects people and how those fighting abroad are not unlike themselves or people they know. Students will also be able to bring into the discussion any experiences they do have with, for example, war or family in the military.

Teachers can prompt students to further consider questions such as: *When there is a broader interest at hand, such as protecting an entire country, does that make death in war understandable? Even for a mother? Should potential causalities be a consideration in decisions to go to war? To what extent?*

Finally, *after* reading the book, teachers might want to revisit these questions and explore if students' original opinions changed once they have read the memoir. Students can practice citing textual evidence to support their opinions and can produce writing that effectively argues their chosen stance.

Helping Students (Re)Form Opinions about Child Solders: The Perpetrators and the Affected

Beah's (2007) memoir intertwines concepts of death, war, and being a child soldier. Because these topics may be new or confusing for students, time should be allotted to explore these three interconnected issues. For example, learning about how often children have been forced to fight in their countries and its prevalence today will help students further see that Beah's (2007) story is an important one, but only one of many, and that this occurrence is a broader social justice issue that warrants more attention.

It is estimated that there are currently tens of thousands of child soldiers participating in various conflicts across the globe (UNICEF, 2017). Teachers can help students to consider questions such as: *What are the perceived benefits of engaging children in war? What might make a child decide to join a fighting group? What choices, if any, do they really have? How were the child soldiers in Beah's book able to kill so readily? How were those who were "rehabilitated" able to move past the events and circumstances that led them to becoming child soldiers?*

The British Red Cross (2018) provides lesson plans specifically geared at helping students understand the plight of child soldiers. Their identified learning outcomes include the following:

• Students will develop the ability to consider other points of view by exploring the thoughts and feelings of another young person.
• Students will recognize how an individual's options might be severely restricted in certain circumstances and require balancing of one evil against another.
• Students will become aware of some of the techniques used to coerce young people into militias, and of the existence of child soldiers (British Red Cross, 2018, n.p.).

The lesson plans on the Red Cross website (see box 12.1) offer scenarios for students to consider and discuss based on documented experiences. For example, students are prompted to imagine that they live in an area where fighting is occurring, and their family learns that one of the groups plans to come in the night and forcibly "recruit" either them or their younger sibling. How would they feel? What would they do?

Students then are called to reflect upon various points of view—the younger sibling, the parents, and so on—and to produce a creative writing piece connected to the topic (British Red Cross, 2018). Reading additional firsthand accounts will help further humanize those affected by war and hopefully break down some of the othering, as mentioned previously, that can occur in a study of such situations.

To further facilitate these connections, however, teachers must accompany the readings and students' writing exercises with critical questions that prompt students to read closely, draw associations, and relate to the narrators. For example, a teacher might ask students: *In what ways are the speakers typical children? What parts of their childhood have they lost? How are their experiences similar to and different from your own?*

Similar to the British Red Cross' (2018) plans, Amnesty International (see box 12.1) provides lesson plans focusing on child soldiers, but specific to Beah's (2007) text and an interview with Beah himself. Including facts, statistics, and a blank map for students to identify countries where children are used in war, this resource provides more discussion prompts and writing and reflection activities. For example, one activity prompts:

> Here are some pictures that were actually drawn by children in Sierra Leone to illustrate their experiences when they were child soldiers. Imagine that you were one of the children who drew one of these pictures. Write a diary of what happened to you on that day. Explain your picture. What are you thinking? (Amnesty, n.d., p. 9)

Beah, himself, says one of the reasons he wrote the book, despite how painful it was to remember what he went through, was to, "expose what continues to happen to a lot of children," and he wants people to realize that "these (child soldiers) are human beings that this is happening to" (Woodrow Wilson Center, 2013). When intentionally explored, stories like Beah's (2007) can deepen outsiders' understandings of their experiences and the conditions and death that plague children soldiers' experiences before, during, and after.

In addition to these suggested classroom activities, students could also conduct their own research projects on a country or war that has been involved child soldiers. Small groups or individual students could research informational texts, such as those containing statistics related to the situation and the setting in which it occurred. They could then compare across contexts and to Beah's (2007) story to identify similarities, such as common storylines or representations of the enemy. This classroom task hones students' research skills as well as strengthens their capacities for assessing sources and integrating information effectively.

While the histories and specifics of each site where child soldiers exist are certainly unique, their interest in these defensive groups would provide students with the knowledge that such is not an anomaly and, through opening their eyes to the fact that this is a widespread phenomenon, hopefully students will feel that this violence must be addressed.

Helping Students (Re)Form Opinions about Global Responsibility through Social Action Projects

In learning about war and the death toll that it often brings, students need to also explore what it means to act. To merely learn about atrocities in the world is not enough, as to educate students without showing them how they can affect change leaves them in a state of helplessness (Boyd, 2017; Downey, 2005). Thus, once students have read Beah's (2007) memoir and engaged with its complex themes, a teacher can pose the question: *What can we do?* This applies to both local and global contexts, as devastating effects related to war are not only abroad, but can often be seen in one's own country, through, for example, the presence of refugees and related policies.

The concept of thinking beyond oneself is a challenging one, especially during adolescence. References in Beah's (2007) text to government relief agencies and nongovernmental organizations (NGOs) (e.g., Children Associated with the WAR [CAW], UNICEF, and various religious organizations) offer students research opportunities to investigate different groups and ways to support those in need on both local and global levels, and Beah's (2007) personal account of various individuals and relief organizations gives readers examples of the vast need and impact that can be made once people recognize that the demand exists.

Similar to the research described earlier but extending it toward action, teachers can therefore task students with researching current global crises (or crises for which there is still a need to assist in the aftermath) and countries in which relief efforts are underway. They can assign small groups of students a region or allow students to investigate and choose their own area of focus.

For example, students might choose to investigate relief efforts surrounding current natural disasters like hurricanes, earthquakes, and typhoons. They might research support for people in countries with a disease outbreak or those countries suffering from severe drought, famine, or lack of food and safe water.

Once students have located a crisis in which they are interested, they can conduct a social action project to in some way enact their responsibility as a global citizen. They could, as mentioned, focus their efforts in the United States, supporting refugees, for example, or they might wish to locate their endeavors abroad, in the space where the crisis occurs. This work will help students develop their own inquiries and take the necessary steps to research them astutely. In determining the problems and needs in an area, it also facilitates students' skills in synthesizing information from multiple sources.

Teachers can follow the *contextualize, organize, act, reflect (COAR)* model for social action projects (Boyd, 2017) as a guide for leading youth through planning and implementing efforts to effect change. Within this framework, students first *contextualize* the problem on which they decide to center their work. This first phase "comprises extensive research on the history of the topic, its manifestations, related legislation, and the key actors involved" (Boyd, 2017, p. 102).

If students are working in a U.S. classroom, it will be important for them to investigate the government's prior and current involvement in the issue as well as potential human rights violations and the United Nations' role in addressing those. This will help inform what they decide to do about the injustices they recognize.

Next, students *organize* an action they wish to take related to the issue. Teachers are vital guides during this step, helping students determine what can be done and if it's within their scope of reach.

Within the milieu of reading Beah's (2007) novel, students' projects might range from raising awareness (Young, 2009) about an area affected by war and death to conducting a campaign for letter writing to government officials (Bomer & Bomer, 2001) to soliciting funds or supplies to be sent for refugees locally. Regardless of the path they determine, the planning commenced at this point is key so that the *action* phase of the project, the next step, is carried out successfully.

Finally, students should *reflect* on their projects, noting their successes and shortcomings and they should "determine how they will continue to address this social issue, answering the question, what's next?" which illustrates "that social change is an ongoing, often iterative process" (Boyd, 2017, p. 103).

Such projects facilitate students' civic literacies (Epstein, 2014), their understandings that the world extends beyond their immediate context. As such, they have an obligation to help those who, most likely dissimilar from them, have to literally fight for their communities and homes. Beah's (2007) memoir offers this opportunity to consider what an individual's duty is, to not just themselves, but also to neighbors, community members, the nation, and beyond.

CAUTIONS AND ADVICE

Talking about war, violence, and displacement can be traumatic for students who have firsthand experiences with similar events. The book describes in detail Beah's (2007) encounters with and the repercussions of violence, war, death, drugs, loss, and feelings of helplessness and despair. Any of these topics can bring up unwanted and difficult feelings and emotions for students who have experienced trauma.

Moreover, it may be easy for students to fall into "othering," and stereotyping. If they have lived a life of safety and relative comfort, it may be easy to judge people, governments, and leaders from places that have civil unrest. It is important for readers not to consume the book as a story of some place far away, but to focus on the humanity that is displayed throughout, making text-to-self connections whenever possible.

Teachers, too, should check their own feelings, emotions, and potential biases on the topics explored in this memoir and do some personal research on the conflict in Sierra Leone, the over 300,000 child soldiers estimated to be fighting in conflicts across the globe today, and ways individuals and organizations can support victims of war. Teachers might even consider sharing with students their initial feelings and beliefs, where they may have come from, and any ways they may have changed through research and reading the book to serve as a model of what it is like to reconsider one's opinions after living vicariously through Beah's (2007) memoir.

CONCLUSION

Beah (2007) claims, "Children have the resilience to outlive their sufferings, if given a chance," and clearly he is proof of this sentiment. His message of hope is a powerful one. Regardless of the trauma or loss one has experienced, this book offers a message that people just might be able to forgive, manage, and move forward with those sufferings.

Beah's (2007) story shows readers that even in darkness, there can be light, and that it is possible to get through the unspeakable, especially with support and thoughtful attention from others. When engaged with stories such as Beah's (2007), youth can discern their own potential to both overcome pain and to participate in social change that addresses such global concerns. Beah's (2007) memoir shows readers that it is possible to resist violence, that it is essential to protect children, and that it is necessary for people to stand up and fight for the vulnerable, and all those who may not have the ability to speak up and fight for themselves.

BOX 12.1   CONNECTED RESOURCES

Woodrow Wilson Center. (2013, October 1). *A long way gone: Memoirs of a boy soldier* [Video file]. Retrieved from https://www.youtube.com/watch?v=17M7ms0kjww

This interview is from the "Dialogue" series of the Woodrow Wilson International Center for Scholars. Twenty-eight minutes in length, the video is of an interview with Beah who speaks about both the book and his life before and after the book was released.

Amnesty International Human Rights in the Curriculum Resource. (n.d.). Amnesty International: Child soldiers. Retrieved from https://www.amnesty.org.uk/files/activities_resource_0.pdf

This website offers lesson plans about child soldiers in general as well as plans specifically connected to Beah's text.

British Red Cross. (2018). Child soldier. Retrieved from https://www.redcross.org.uk/get-involved/teaching-resources/teaching-pages/child-soldier

This website provides lesson plans and teaching resources to help students better understand how war can affect children.

The Ishmael Beah Foundation. (2014). Retrieved from http://beta.beahfound.org/

This is the website for the organization Beah founded focusing on "helping children affected by war reintegrate into society and improve their lives," and may serve as an inspiration for other ways that students can get involved in their communities and abroad.

DePrince, M. (2014). *Taking flight: From war orphan to star ballerina.* New York, NY: Random House.

Also a child from war-torn Sierra Leone, Mikaela DePrince's autobiography gives another opportunity for students to consider war, death, violence, and resilience. By reading two very different accounts of the same conflict, both written by young authors.

REFERENCES

Beah, I. (2007). *A long way gone: Memoirs of a boy soldier*. New York, NY: Sarah Crichton Books.

Bomer, R., & Bomer, K. (2001). *For a better world: Reading and writing for social action*. Portsmouth, NH: Heinemann.

Boyd, A. S. (2017). *Social justice literacies in the English classroom: Teaching practice in action*. New York, NY: Teachers College Press.

Downey, A. L. (2005). The transformative power of drama: Bringing literature and social justice to life. *English Journal, 95*(1), 33–38.

Epstein, S. E. (2014). *Teaching civic literacy projects: Student engagement with social problems*. New York, NY: Teachers College Press.

The Teacher Toolkit. (n.d.) Four corners. Retrieved from http://www.theteachertool kit.com/index.php/tool/four-corners

UNICEF. (2017). At least 65,000 children released from armed forces and groups over the last 10 years. Retrieved from https://www.unicef.org/media/media_94892. html

Wormeli, R. (2005). The human continuum. *Association for Supervision and Curriculum Development*. Retrieved from http://www.ascd.org/publications/ books/104014/chapters/Human-Continuum.aspx

Young, S. L. B. (2009). Breaking the silence: Critical literacy and social action. *English Journal, 98*(4), 109–15.

Chapter 13

Teaching the Act of Witnessing in *Maus* and *Night*

Crystal Chen Lee and Cathlin Goulding

According to the U.S. Holocaust Memorial Museum (2017), teaching historical accounts such as the Holocaust allows students to gain awareness of the complexity of historical accounts, and to examine the historical, social, religious, political, and economic factors that may impact democratic moral values.

As stated on the website, it is the belief that when students learn about such historical accounts, students can "understand that it is the responsibility of citizens in any society . . . and know when to react" ("Teaching about the Holocaust," 2017). Such teachings were grounded on the assumption that when students read such historical accounts, they will learn to seek social justice, to be responsible citizens, and to be advocates for human rights (Adorno, 1998; Friedlander, 1979; Ragland & Rosenstein, 2014; Westervelt, 2015).

Policymakers and educators believe that reading and learning from historical accounts translate to the act of "bearing witness," or otherwise, "taking responsibility" for ensuring that such traumas may never happen again (Simon & Eppert, 1997). According to Felman and Laub (1992), witnessing involves "taking responsibility in speech for history, or becoming a catalyst or agent of the process of awareness and reception of the trauma by others" (p. 213).

However, few resources and research studies on how teachers and students have actually responded to the reading of historical accounts have been conducted. Particularly, what is the response in *reading about and talking about death in historical accounts? How do educators facilitate talking about death in historical accounts?* The assumption that students "learn to seek social justice" or to "be responsible citizens" after such readings have not been clearly articulated nor proven.

Historical accounts are defined as "accounts that convey multiple expressive forms of historical substance and significance of prior events and experiences" (Simon & Eppert, 1997, p. 176). The retelling of nonfiction experiences can take on various forms such as diaries, eye-witness statements, documentaries, testimonies, or fictionalized stories. Such accounts often explore particular traumas or reveal particular injustices such as racism, slavery, or genocide in historical times. However, the process in which the teaching and learning of these traumas and the emotions associated with the act of witnessing are often left unexplored.

SUMMARY OF *NIGHT* AND *MAUS*

This book chapter is a practical resource for English language arts (ELA) teachers and teacher educators to teach the curricular content and the emotions associated with death in discussing Holocaust literature, specifically *Night* and *Maus*. This chapter encourages teachers to utilize the use of dialogue and an analysis of multimodal texts to process and talk about death in historical accounts. These tools and applications illuminate how analyzing historical accounts involve readers in the very act of witnessing the testimonies and stories surrounding the Holocaust.

Night, written in 1956, stands as a seminal work of literature through the first-person account of Elie Wiesel and his father's experience in the Nazi German concentration camps at Auschwitz and Buchenwald in 1944–1945, at the height of the Holocaust during World War II. The slim volume begins with a telling of a young Wiesel's education in Jewish mysticism.

In this volume, Wiesel (2006) writes about the death of God and the dehumanization he witnesses as a prisoner of the camp. As his father's physical and mental state declines, Wiesel reflects on the inversion of the parent-child relationship and begins to feel shame about his resentfulness in being a caregiver to his father. In this searing personal memoir, Wiesel (2006) conveys the complexities and hardships of witnessing death and injustice as a teenager.

Maus, written thirty years later after *Night* in 1986, offers a different approach to witnessing, one that tells the story of the Holocaust through the method of graphic novel. Written by cartoonist Art Spiegelman, a second-generation Holocaust survivor, *Maus* weaves the story of the Holocaust and the Jewish American narrator's quest and struggle to witness this account. The frame-tale timeline begins in 1978 in New York City and depicts Spiegelman (1997) interviewing his father about his experiences as a Polish Jew and Holocaust survivor.

In a postmodernist technique that represents Jews as mice, Germans as cats, Poles as pigs, and American soldiers as dogs, Spiegelman (1997) tells his parents' story of the years leading up to World War II and their liberation from the concentration camps. Much of the story also interweaves Spiegelman's difficult relationship with his father and the absence of his mother after the war.

WITNESSING AS A PEDAGOGICAL APPROACH

This chapter presents an ELA unit that juxtaposes the reading and analysis of *Night* by Elie Wiesel (2006) and *Maus* by Art Spiegelman (1997) through dialoguing about witnessing and death. In correlation with literacy standards that ask students to analyze multiple genres, compare and contrast accounts, and illustrate multimodal texts, this pairing of *Night* and *Maus* allows the students to witness the Holocaust through various mediums.

In doing so, teachers and teacher educators might enlist a pedagogy of witnessing—the act of witnessing death through first, second, and third accounts. The chapter offers lessons that allow students to discuss the limitations of witnessing while learning how to process particular emotions through two genres written on the same historical event.

This chapter is an inquiry into how educators might negotiate, disrupt, and investigate a powerful undercurrent set by current Holocaust literature in classrooms: Does *reading about death* necessitate or lead to an ethical action? Our essential questions include the following:

- What does it mean to witness? What do these genres offer in reading about, talking about, and processing about death that occurred?
- Who is the real witness? What is our role as teachers and students who are witnesses to historical deaths in the Holocaust? Will there always be a failure to witnessing, and what does it entail?
- How can students understand the limitations of witnessing, and what does it mean to read a partial account?

In teaching about the complicated nature of civic action and emotional disruption, multiple stakeholders should be involved in the discussion. Within this book chapter, the act of witnessing requires the nature of investigating the kinds of knowledge narratives produce. Part of the process of moving toward democratic action is first recognizing the inequities and partialities produced in narratives. Teachers and students might articulate the *unspoken* and the *spoken* in order to contribute to the study of teaching historical accounts in English education (Simon & Eppert, 1997).

In the case of genocide, death is systematic and motivated by entrenched racial and exclusionary ideologies. Sanctioned by the nation-state, it often involves stripping a targeted group of legal rights and their eventual sequestering into the concentration camp or other confinement sites, spaces in which atrocities and mass murder become possible. An attempt to grasp at these crimes has long been the project of artists, historians, and educators, whose work concerns the memorialization and documentation of the Holocaust and other periods of historical violence.

Elie Wiesel (2006) and Art Spiegelman (1997) use two distinctive literary forms to recount their personal and familial experiences during the Holocaust. While one is a memoir and the other a graphic novel, both texts broach the questions of remembrance, representation, and the transgenerational obligation to bear witness.

These next sections will describe how *Night* and *Maus* are forms of witnessing to the Holocaust, highlighting each author's distinctive literary and graphic techniques. Next, specific pedagogical strategies are detailed on how readers can, too, inhabit the role of witness to history during the reading of these books. For *Night*, the strategy of using dialogue journals to spur shared acts of witnessing is described; alternatively, for *Maus*, teaching the language of comics and conducting a visual analysis of the graphic novel are outlined. Finally, a project called *Toolboxes for Witnessing* is offered as a summative assessment.

Elie Wiesel's *Night*: Bringing Language to Bear on Mass Violence

Reading a book like Elie Wiesel's *Night* (2006) requires a certain forbearance from learners, requiring a confrontation with acts of violence, which stretch the limits of intelligibility. On route to the concentration camp in a cattle car, a woman screams at a prescient vision of fire in the distance. "I see a fire!" she says. "I see flames, huge flames!" (Wiesel, 2006, p. 25).

In another part of the novel, a boy with an angelic face is hung on the gallows for all prisoners to view. Viewing the scene, a young Wiesel (2006) overhears someone ask aloud: "Where is merciful God, where is he?" (p. 64). In response, Wiesel (2006) thinks to himself: "Where He is? This is where— hanging here from this gallows" (p. 65).

What, then, do teachers do in the seconds after reading these passages that depict or portend death? In the moments after the text and images settle in, do they allow for silence? Do they encourage talk? Should students write in their journals for a few moments and then share with a partner? Or should the words soak in and not be tainted with analysis? And what are the pedagogical possibilities, the gains, and the losses in each decision?

Teaching *Night* involves a recognition of its descriptive potency and the purposive use of language as a vehicle for bearing witness. In his literary works, Wiesel sought to address and resist the annihilative effects of totalitarian regimes. The violence of the concentration camps and the bureaucratic organization that expedited such acts exceeded linguistic and psychic frameworks for understanding.

Acknowledging this lacuna, Wiesel (1985) explains in an essay on his writing process that he "could never express in words, coherent, intelligible words, our experience of madness on an absolute scale" (para. 7). The kinds of violence experienced in the camps, he writes, "negated all other language" (para. 8). Yet, despite the impossibility of representing the camps in language, Wiesel strives to describe the camps out of a responsibility to those who died. "It was the last wish of the dead," he explains (para. 8).

In the face of representational challenges, Wiesel (2006) describes his family's forced removal from Sighet, Hungary, and the events that transpired in the concentration camps in spare and crystalline prose. Scenes of flames and gallows are followed with commentary of clear-eyed, harrowing concision. After the young boy is hung on the gallows, for example, Wiesel (2006) only notes: "That night, the soup tasted of corpses" (p. 65).

Wiesel (2006) ends scenes with a stark portentousness, with a terseness that, in turn, demands a readerly response. While teachers have a range of pedagogical choices in cultivating these responses, the austerity of Wiesel's (2006) textual compactness can be complemented and worked through in shared, free-flowing conversation among students.

Collaborative Writing as Collective Witnessing

What happens when the act of witnessing is dispersed or shared among a group of readers? Dialogue journals, a common practice in literacy instruction, are one approach that teachers can use to spur acts of collective witnessing, in which students write in collaboration with one another. Dialogue journals reframe reading about death as an intersubjective activity that happens with and alongside others.

First, teachers should assemble a set of notebooks or prepare a digital writing space designated solely for responding to *Night*. Second, teachers should plan "dialogue" partners ahead of time. One way to set up these partnerships is to create cross-class dialogue pairs or groups of three or four, in which students from one class write to students from another class or school.

In order to create these groups, teachers might consider a range of academic and social factors, such as cultivating conversations across different genders and home languages or pairing students with great textual fluency with learners who might need more practice with writing paragraph length text.

For the duration of reading *Night*, teachers should distribute the dialogue journals and provide ample time for students to write responses to the novel and to their partner. At the initial part of the dialogue journals, teachers can give students a series of prompts to guide student writing.

For the first entry, the entry can be informal and introductory. Students can discuss their identity, what communities they belong to, hobbies, interests, classes, or feelings about school. Dialogue partners should not rush these introductory entries, as they are critical community building step before beginning the work of shared witnessing. *Night* is intended as a disturbing provocation for the reader, an empathic tracing of one's own experiences against that of a young Wiesel.

Given the intensity of the reading experience, a certain measure of trust, established through shared affiliations and overlapping identity markers, is one precondition of collaborative witnessing. Taking some time to get to know each other relieves some of the trepidations of dialoguing with someone who may be a stranger or a mere acquaintance; it also sets the stage for self-revelation and vulnerability while reading and thus witnessing the events in *Night*.

After the first entry, teachers can let students guide their own responses and be responsive to one another. Sometimes, teachers may wish to take a key scene from the book as an entry point for the writing. The final line of the book, for example, where Wiesel (2006) describes looking into the mirror and seeing a corpse, can jumpstart a journal dialogue about what parts of Wiesel died during his ordeal. If needed, the following prompts might stir journal entries:

- What do you think of the book so far?
- Do you have any questions about the story or the writing?
- Do you see any connections to anything you have learned before?
- Make a list of events that have happened so far.
- What is disturbing? What stands out?

Students can have a set time for writing in the journal, such as five to ten minutes at the beginning of each class period. Regardless of the time length, students should work on responding directly to the other writers in a sustained dialogue: making predictions, asking questions of their writing partners, making connections and citing the text, generating comments, and clarifying confusing aspects of the text.

Significantly, as the writerly relationship between the pairs develops, so does the process of collective witnessing. Teachers should check the journals with some regularity, highlighting key moments in their conversation and noticing where students support or challenge their discoveries within the text.

Dialogue journals shift readers from a state of singularity and loneliness to a shared experience of encountering death. In the collaborative act of reading and writing, the act of witnessing becomes a collective encounter, one that in which readers are not left alone with the kind of knowledge that Wiesel asks them to confront.

Art Spiegelman's *Maus*: Loss and Violence
Distilled in Graphic Forms

Different from *Night*, Spiegelman's (1997) graphic novel is a study in sec-
ondhand witnessing. As the son of a Holocaust survivor, Spiegelman uses the
graphic novel form to recreate his parents' experiences in the camps, shifting
back and forth between World War II Poland and the present-day in Rego
Park, Queens.

Moreover, Spiegelman (1997) grapples with the impossibility of representing these very experiences, drawing himself in as a character who speculates
on his own writing process. Rather than drawing human figures, Spiegelman
(1997) radically elected to use animals as stand-ins for people: the titular
mice for Jews, cats for Germans denizens and Nazi guards, pigs for Polish
characters, and dogs for American soldiers. *Maus* poses a unique literacy
task for readers: it asks readers to bear witness to genocide through a series
of symbol-laden figures.

Conscious of the powerful role of the image, Spiegelman (1997) chose to
draw his characters in simple, unadorned line drawings. "In making *Maus*
I found myself drawing every panel, every figure, over and over—obses-
sively—so as to pare it down to an essence," explained Spiegelman (1994,
p. 46). "Every panel had to become the shortest definition of itself" (p. 46).
Reading *Maus* in the classroom can be a generative opportunity to teach students the processual and psychic labors of representing genocide and our own
role in bringing an interpretative lens to such texts.

Visual Forms of Witnessing: The Process of Abstraction

To help students engage with *Maus*, teachers can conduct a quick review of
the comics' lexicon. In comics, graphic forms become substitutes for real
objects and beings through a process of abstraction. Comics theorist Scott
McCloud (1993, p. 29) describes a face relieved of realistic features: Eyes are
stripped of lashes, pupils consolidate into two dots, the curves of the mouth
reduced to a straight line, and the face shaved into a circle. A complex and
highly specific portrait of the human face is reduced to a series of simple
lines.

The image, bereft of its specificities, becomes a universal vessel for identification. In its abstraction, the image is now an "icon" and serves as an opening for many possible meanings and interpretations.

Let students know that they will start off with a brief introduction to comic
book theory and symbolism in literary texts. Teachers can begin a lesson on
icons by asking students to respond to the following prompt: "If you were to
draw yourself as an animal, what would it be? Take a few minutes to identify

an animal, write out the reasoning for this choice, and draw yourself as this animal." Then, teachers might elicit students' responses and ask them to describe the underlying meaning this animal symbolizes.

Next, teachers should spend some time demonstrating and digesting icons, or images that have taken on symbolic meaning and messages. The communicative power of abstracted images is a familiar and ubiquitous part of a media and advertising-saturated society. Projecting an image of a real human heart against the heart-as-icon in emoji form can quickly demonstrate a complex theory of visual representation. The Statue of Liberty could be swiftly read as a stand-in for freedom, immigration, or democracy. Animated figures like Mickey Mouse, who is darkly referenced in *Maus'* epigraph, represent early childhood, spontaneity, and consumption.

Having students view and analyze a series of icons is a provocative exercise to jumpstart a discussion of symbolic meanings. Icons like architecture fixtures, political figures or celebrities, animations, or advertising logos all work well for this activity. Teachers can project these images, pausing after each to brainstorm the larger conceptual meanings the icons relay and allowing ample room for contestation and critique of these meanings.

To expose students to more visual forms of representation, it is also worth considering showing footage from *The Eternal Jew* (U.S. Holocaust Memorial Museum, n.d.), a Nazi propaganda film that frames Jews as vermin through footage of swarming rats and polemical voiceover. A viewing of this film puts students in a better position to analyze how Spiegelman (1997) both utilized and inverted the meaning of the mouse within his own work.

Students can now shift to an exploration of abstracted figures in *Maus*. Some useful questions to begin this conversation are as follows:

- Why do you think Spiegelman chose to use comic book to tell the story of the Holocaust?
- What ideas could Spiegelman convey about the Holocaust that he wouldn't have been about to do in another art form?
- What advantages do comics give in telling painful stories?

After some discussion, ask students to rummage through the text and chart a list of icons from *Maus* and their larger social, political, philosophical, or emotional interpretations. A chart like shown in table 13.1 can serve as a scaffold for their analysis, asking students to plot out a series of five or six iconic objects, figures, or images they find in the text.

Remind them to choose carefully and select icons that they believe represent a powerful meaning or idea. Students will often select the animals-as-humans as the icons of choice; however, many will ferret out less pronounced ones, such as utensils or other objects that were key to survival in the camps.

Table 13.1.   A Chart for Students' Investigations of Icons in Art Spiegelman's *Maus*

Icon	Pg. #	Sketch of the Icon	Meaning: What Does the Icon Signify or Mean? What Larger Ideas, Beliefs, Political Ideas, or Feelings Does the Icon Represent?
Example: The number tattooed on Vladek's and other prisoners' arms.	28		The tattooed numbers on the wrists of prisoners represent how the Jews were less than human in the eyes of the Nazis. It shows how the Nazis saw the Jews as numbers rather than people. The tattoos symbolize how the Nazis carried out the extermination of Jews with a bureaucratic coldness.

Once they have charted a selection of icons, pass out colorful squares of paper. On this square, students should compose a detailed analysis of this icon, explaining what the icon figuratively represents, and why it is important to the graphic novel as a whole (see figure 13.1 for a model). They should also trace or draw their icon on this square. Teachers can affix a "quilt" of these squares on the wall, peppering the classroom with visual cues from Spiegelman's (1997) text.

Their collective set of icons becomes reminders of the complex work of reducing genocide into narrativized format. Each line stroke in the graphic novel, their repetition, and unique formations across the panels reflect the restraint of their maker. The icons furrow into the reader's mind in an iterative process of captivation and receptivity: Vladek Spiegelman's glasses, slipping down his nose; Anja's anxious fleeing from the prison guard; the knife-like teeth and slit eyes of the Nazi cats. The icons' symbolic weightiness and levity enlist readers into the often unresolved and disquieting states of bearing witness to a violent past.

The Toolbox for Witnessing Project

Teachers may wish to assign a summative assessment after finishing a reading of *Night* or *Maus*. Recognizing that witnessing is always a partial and unfinished act, teachers can ask students to create a "toolbox" that reflects starting points or initiations for acting as a witness. As a final assessment to reading either *Maus* or *Night*, students can construct "toolboxes of witnessing," that integrate and present a key theme from the texts using multiple kinds of media.

The mask is a key icon throughout *Maus*: Art Spiegelman wears a mask while struggling to draw his family's experiences in the death camps. Art's therapist has a mask while helping Art work through his feelings about his father.

Wearing a mask offers characters concealment from danger or recognition. In other cases, masks indicate a self-protective impulse in moments of emotional vulnerability. The masks symbolize barriers between characters, or their inability to understand or embrace one another.

The mask is a projection, a persona put forth in order to disguise inner feelings, identities, and personhood. The mask also serves to underline impenetrable nature of the book's subject, the Holocaust, and the extent to which we are strangers to one another, even the people to whom we are most closely associated.

Figure 13.1.   A Teacher Exemplar Analysis of an Icon in Art Spiegelman's Maus

This project will ask students to make sense of the experience of witnessing and the challenges and ethical obligations it raises. The *Toolbox for Witnessing* project asks students to draw upon the studied texts and create a "toolbox" with elements that reflect a notion of witnessing and its potential implications.

Using class time, ask students to brainstorm around the words "witness to history." Then, students should take some time to jot down: *Who* is the witness to history, *what* is the responsibility of the witness to history, *how* does the process of witnessing unfold, and in *what places*, *spaces*, and *times* does the role of the witness play a significant role?

After some brainstorming, students can begin work on creating their toolboxes. Teachers might find it useful to create a checklist or worksheet, which names all of the requirements and gives students some space for planning their designs. Their toolbox will be an actual container that holds all their "tools" for witnessing. It can be a box with a new design or aesthetic, a hollowed-out book, a sewn or fabric-based object, a frame, or any other kind of physical receptacle.

Inside of the box, teachers should ask students to locate and creatively arrange a series of objects or texts. Students can include a series of photographs or images related to the theme. Often times, these images can be related to the specific historical context of the Holocaust but also can connect to other genocides or atrocities students have independently researched. Found poems (created from *Night* or *Maus*) or quotations from the books also make moving contributions to the box.

In teaching students to trace a theme, the vessel should have a background, which successfully interconnects the quotations, found poetry, and photos in a visually pleasing and thoughtful manner. Students might create collages of images, drawings, patterns, word walls, or blocks of colored paper as a background. Finally, the toolbox should contain a clear suggestion on the place of the witness in addressing mass violence. Students can use words, drawings, or photographs of activists or artists convey this idea (see figure 13.2 for an example of a toolbox).

Students should compose a one-page reflection on their subject, project, and work process. The reflection should explain each of their components and how they fit together and the message they hope people take away from the project. Aligned with literacy standards to analyze literature in various modes, teachers can also do an art gallery with all of the students' toolboxes, giving students ample time to see their fellow students' project and reflect upon them.

CAUTIONS AND ADVICE

Undergirding this unit is a caution that learners can never fully witness the narrative encounters of the Holocaust. Educators and students can only be critical witnesses of the human experience, as textual knowledge cannot represent nor make comprehensible the true violence and losses of the camps. The first step is acknowledging this limitation; the second is that in recognizing this limitation and discussing such limitations, being able to name injustices in order to move toward civic action that seeks a more equitable and just society.

In taking caution when teaching about the Holocaust, examining the strategies provided by the U.S. Holocaust Museum's Guidelines for Teaching the Holocaust (see box 13.1) can be of some utility for teachers. Strategies include practical tips such as "avoid simple answers to complex questions," "strive for precision of language," "avoid comparisons of pain," "do not romanticize history," and "contextualize history."

Figure 13.2.   An Exemplar Toolbox for Witnessing

CONCLUSION

This chapter is just one step in reconceptualizing the teaching of historical accounts in the English classroom—an approach to deconstruct the "power dynamics that lay behind the ways we . . . construe the world" (Berlak, 2004, p. 116). Coconstructed discussions and the analysis of graphic forms are only some of the techniques and tools to teach historical accounts. Two final questions might be posed: "What do students gain through the teaching of trauma and the discussing death? What role, if any, do these readings play in teaching students to be social justice activists?"

By approaching the thresholds of witnessing, readers may engage as witnesses with an obligation and ethical warrant to create a more just future society. After all, teaching the act of witnessing necessitates students, teachers, and researchers to collaboratively deconstruct such notions together as critical witnesses of the human experience.

BOX 13.1   CONNECTED RESOURCES

Pixton Comics. (2018). Retrieved from www.pixton.com

  A reliably functional and accessible web platform to create multi-paneled comics with a range of customizable characters, backdrops, and props.

McCloud, S. (1993). *Understanding comics: The invisible art*. New York, NY: HarperCollins Publishers.

  A key text to teaching the history and theoretical underpinnings of comics.

United States Holocaust Memorial Museum. (n.d.). Lessons and curricular resources. Retrieved from https://www.ushmm.org/educators/lesson-plans

  Historical documents and materials used for teaching the Holocaust.

United States Holocaust Memorial Museum. (2017, December 20). Guidelines on teaching about the Holocaust. Retrieved from https://www.ushmm.org/educators/teaching-about-the-holocaust/general-teaching-guidelines

  General teaching guidelines on cautions and advice for teaching about the Holocaust including resources and "what to do" and "what not to do."

REFERENCES

Adorno, T. W. (1998). *Critical models: Interventions and catchwords*. New York, NY: Columbia University Press.

Berlak, A. (2004). Confrontation and pedagogy: Cultural secrets, trauma, and emotion in anti-oppressive pedagogies. In M. Boler (Ed.), *Democratic dialogue in education: Troubling speech, disturbing silence* (pp. 123–44). New York, NY: Peter Lang.

Felman, S., & Laub, D. (1992). *Testimony: Crisis of witnessing in literature, psycho-analysis, and history.* New York, NY: Routledge.

McCloud, S. (1993). *Understanding comics: The invisible art.* New York, NY: HarperCollins.

Ragland, R. G., & Rosenstein, D. (2014). Holocaust education: Analysis of curricula and frameworks: A case study of Illinois. *The Social Studies, 105*(4), 175–83.

Simon, R., & Eppert, C. (1997). Remembering obligation: Pedagogy and the witnessing of testimony of historical trauma. *Canadian Journal of Education, 22*(2), 175–91.

Spiegelman, A. (1994, January 17). Mightier than the sorehead. *The Nation, 258*(2), 45–54.

Spiegelman, A. (1997). *Maus: A survivor's tale* (Vols. 1–2). New York, NY: Pantheon Books.

United States Holocaust Memorial Museum. (2017, December 20). Guidelines for teaching about the Holocaust. Retrieved from https://www.ushmm.org/educators/teaching-about-the-holocaust/general-teaching-guidelines

Westervelt, E. (Host). (2015, March 1). Teaching the Holocaust: New approaches for a new generation [Radio broadcast episode]. Retrieved from https://www.npr.org/sections/ed/2015/02/20/387654149/teaching-the-holocaust-new-approaches-for-a-new-generation

Wiesel, E. (1985, April 14). Why I write: Making no become yes. *New York Times Book Review*, 13–14.

Wiesel, E. (2006). *Night.* New York, NY: Farrar, Straus and Giroux.

Chapter 14

When a Character Dies: Comfort and Discomfort in *Refugee* Book Groups

Sarah J. Donovan

It's the week before winter break, and my seventh-grade reading class is meeting in book groups to decide who is bringing which snack to their discussion tomorrow. I listen in as they negotiate fruit snacks, chips, and even pie, yes pie.

"Okay, everyone," I say. "Let's find our reading spots and finish the books for tomorrow's discussion. If you've already finished, review your role to select passages for the discussion."

As students find their place in the room and books, I take out my notebook to begin reading conferences. I work my way through the rows and tables to find the next reader, kneel down to have our whisper-conference, and just as I am about to begin, I hear a gasp.

Nate (all names pseudonyms) is holding his book, *Refugee* by Alan Gratz (2017), in one hand and waving down a student with the other, mouth and eyes wide open. His classmate and book group member, Carrie, scurries over to Nate, but Nate is already thumbing through the remaining chapters. Each chapter begins with the name of one of three characters, their location, the year, and how many days they still need to travel to arrive in their new home. His quick investigation confirms what he thought.

"Are you on that part?" Carrie whispers, kneeling next to Nate's desk. "Let me see. I don't want to ruin it."

Nate points to the last paragraph on page 291, the part where Josef's mother, Rachel Landau, must choose one of her children to live and one to die. Nate realizes that Josef dies, and Carrie sits beside him as the news settles in.

Paulo Freire and Donaldo Macedo (1987) write, "Reading the world always precedes reading the word, and reading the word implies continually reading the world. . . . We can go further and say that reading the word is not preceded by merely reading the world, but by a certain form of writing it or rewriting it, that is, of transforming it by means of conscious, practical work" (p. 23).

In a globalized world, multivoiced stories offer teens new landscapes for discovery, places where they can learn to read the world and imagine its transformation. Some such landscapes represent the most egregious acts of humankind: the Holocaust. For decades, English classrooms have been reading Holocaust literature; teen readers bear witness to atrocities and resilience in powerful literary works. However, the human rights violations across the world persist, and are those stories heard in English classrooms? The answer will be "no" unless teachers bring them into the classroom.

Teachers continue to bear witness to the stories of modern atrocities—stories never meant to be heard because they come from oppressed peoples, stories of being caught in the crossfire of warring nations as people commute to work, attend school, and practice music. Death is part of these stories. People die, and the people who live can tell the harrowing stories, and young adult authors taking up these historical and contemporary human rights issues in novels make accessible to teens the implications of global conflicts, which include death.

In the act of reading such stories (perhaps from the safety of classrooms), teachers and students make visible, make heard stories of lives lived beyond their own, and just maybe these students will take up the work of imagining a better world.

There is much to discover about why and how international atrocities occur (and continue). Because teens are growing into a globalized world, they must learn to read the rhetoric of progress and development that accepts "collateral damage" in the form of displaced persons, refugee crises, and mass murder. Alan Gratz's (2017) *Refugee* uncovers the far-reaching implications of political unrest across landscapes and across time, for the trauma of war lives in the branches of the family tree. Authors can often do the work teachers and reporters cannot—they make accessible the world in their craft of the word.

SUMMARY OF *REFUGEE*

In *Refugee*, Alan Gratz (2017) tells the story of three. Josef is a Jewish boy in 1930s Nazi Germany. Isabel is a Cuban girl in 1944. Mahmoud is a Syrian boy in 2015. Separated by continents and decades, they each leave home with family and endure an arduous journey to escape persecution—only the journey proves just as dangerous as the homes they left, and not every family member survives.

The prose is clean, direct alternating points of view in each chapter. Josef, Isabel, and Mahmoud are on boats for most of the journey, and the reader certainly feels the waves of their journey navigating the temporal and spatial shifts in the narrative. The story is not overly didactic in "telling" the reader about the political and social violence; in fact, Hitler, Castro, and al-Assad, while always pressing on the characters, are specters hovering in the white spaces (where teen readers can do further inquiry).

The novel opens the conversation about policy regarding refugees and why some countries welcome while others close their borders. Literary representation does much more than convey information about the world. It moves those who read to feel, to imagine, and, in some cases, to act.

A COOPERATIVE READING APPROACH

Reading preferences are personal. The reading experience is also personal because it cannot be duplicated. Nobody can read a book for another because once the text enters a reader's consciousness, the reader is changed and carries the imprint of the story viscerally and intellectually.

Reading is also social. A writer created a text to share with others, and readers encounter that text with their own experiences only to be forever changed by that encounter, which does not cease to exist once the book is closed, especially if that experience is shared with others in discussions and reviews. In a book group, the personal experience of the text will transform. One reader's interpretation or emotional response will be confronted or shaped by another's.

In a book group, there is a chance that what someone else felt or noticed or loved or hated will impact other's understanding of what that book did and can do. Maybe a reader is invited (or forced) to read a passage again to experience the scene anew, and maybe, this re-experiencing is unwelcome, but maybe this re-experiencing unveils a new understanding of the text. The social experience, including the relationships with fellow readers, is then carried in hearts and minds. This is a beautiful communal experience that exists because of the personal *and* the social interacting.

But here is, in my view, the beauty of a book group: the book discussion has the potential to reveal a side of fellow readers that you have not glimpsed until that moment one tells a story of how a passage helped him or her remember his or her father's death or his or her school bully or any moment in life a fellow group member did not experience. And in that moment, the group members are positioned to respond with sympathy, compassion, and comfort. They become witnesses to how a book moves readers in different ways; and they become witnesses to one another's lives.

When, in *Refugee*, Nate realized that Josef had died, Carrie was there to sit alongside him to process the reading experience and comfort him as she knew how, which was to kneel beside his desk and let him talk. Perhaps I, as the teacher, could have done that, too, but it wasn't me that Nate looked for when he made the discovery, it was the people who he had been meeting with for the past three weeks. Discussions can transform experiences of books but also experiences with one another. Book groups are more intimate than whole-class discussions offering productive tension and much needed comfort that can only happen in a small group.

The *Refugee* book group was the first group reading experience of the school year and junior high for Nate, Carrie, and their group members. They were all from different elementary schools, so students did lots of informal small group work for the first couple months of school in preparation for the formal book groups I planned to launch second quarter. Here is my protocol for book group discussions.

Setting Up Small Group Discussions

Begin by setting up groups of five readers strategically so that students can develop relationships with classmates from different schools. In groups, students set the page goals for the three meetings. Together, they look at their calendars and decide if they want to divide the book in equal parts, or if one week they read fewer pages because of projects from other classes.

Teachers can create role sheets for students to use as guides during their reading experience so that they had topic-specific passages and page numbers to discuss. For example, to draw on lessons about connotation and nuance of language, teachers can develop a role sheet called "word connotator." This person's responsibility is to notice words that are unfamiliar, interesting, or even powerful.

On the role sheet, the student writes the word, the page number, the denotation, and then the connotation or how that word relates to the character, setting, conflict, and themes in the book. When the group meets, this group member would bring up the word and ask the group how they think the word relates to or was symbolic of certain ideas in the book. The example in table 14.1 shows how instructive a focus on language can be while also making accessible settings and cultures unfamiliar to some students using a connation role sheet.

Table 14.1.   Student Example of Word Connotator of *Refugee* (pp. 1–75)

Word	Sentence with Page Number in MLA Style	Denotation	Connotation: Positive, Negative, Mixed; to Which Character, Conflict, or Setting Does It Relate
Kristallnacht	"They called it Kristallnacht, the Night of Broken Glass" (5).	When Nazis attacked Jewish people in Germany	Negative. Relates the night when Hitler began physically destroying the homes of Jews—relates to Josef in Germany.
Busker	"Buskers played rumbas, guitars, and drums" (11).	The act of performing in public places for tips	Positive. Musicians playing instruments in public is positive—relates to Isabel in Cuba.
Daesh	"In some places women were being stoned and killed for not covering up their entire bodies, especially in areas controlled by Daesh" (66).	ISIS	Negative. If they killed women for not "covering up". . . . negative—relates to Mahmoud in Syria.
Yarmulke	"There were a hundred men, probably more, all wearing yarmulkes on their heads and white and black tallisims" (75).	A skull cap worn in public by Orthodox Jewish men	Positive. Because they are showing that Hitler can't control them or their religion.
al-Qaeda	"The Free Syrian Army And al-Qaeda are fighting there now" (69).	Militant terrorist group	Negative. The terror relates to Mahmoud's home and why he can't stay.
Radical	"Mahmoud and his family planned to stay as far away from Daesh as possible, but the radical fighters were coming farther and farther into Syria every day" (66).	Advocating complete political or social change, extreme or progressive section of a party	Negative. Relates to ISIS, which is not positive and is why there are refugees like Mahmoud.

Your Name: Sample				BOOK GROUP #1
Title: Refugee		Author: Alan Gratz		PAGES 1 to 75

SUPPORTING CASTER

Names of Supporting Characters	Detail: age, personality, good/bad, relationship with main character Advice he or she gives; conflicts he or she causes	page
Joseph	12, bold, brave → talking to the Nazis	4
Ruth	6, nice relationship w/Joseph; gets nervous; whines a lot	43
Rachel (mom)	Protective. When Joseph says he's a man, the Nazis threaten him, but Mom stands up to the Nazis.	4
Isabel	11, "lanky arms and legs" Caring → she feeds the kittens	7
Iván	12, Isabel's brother. Supportive → helps Isabel care for her secret pet kitten	8
Mahmoud	12, survival Strategy → try to stay invisible. War has made him nervous, twitchy, paranoid	12-13
Waleed	10, brother of Mahmoud "like a robot" because of the war	13
Klaus	same age as Joseph. 12 Had a good relationship with Joseph but forced to to join Hitler Youth → mean to	23

Draw 3 characters who most interact with the main character(s) but do not have a central role; use your character notes to capture a long shot with a typical setting where that character would be in the background.

Figure 14.1. Supporting Caster Example

Another person's job is Supporting Caster: to notice character interactions or passages where two or more characters were engaged in conversation, this reader brings passages to the group to discuss how character interactions impact characters' decisions or events. Other roles include typical literature circle roles like Discussion Leader and Setting Mapper. See figure 14.1 for

Title: REFUGEE   Author: Alan Gratz   PAGES 75 to 157

SETTING MAPPER

For each chapter, track the setting. What happens in those places -- conflict, advice, discoveries? Are the characters interacting, new characters introduced, the main character is alone? Why might that be?

Chapter or pages	Place: building, whose home, street, hospital, park, city, country, state	time of year, season, how much time has passed	What's going on? Who is there and how are they interacting?	Mood words in the chapter (words the author is using to make you feel, gives you a sense of what's happening or going to happen in this scene)	Symbolism: what does this place symbolize (safety, family, peace, racism, freedom, other)
74-80	Somewhere on the Atlantic ocean	1939... 8 days from home	More Jews. Renata, Evelyne, Josefs mom, dad, & sister.	Afraid, desperately	I think it Symbolize culture because Josef becoming a man
81-86	the straits of florida... Some where North of Cuba	1994... 1 day from home	Isabel's family. Neighbors & others. And the are leaving Cuba	frowning	I think racism because they have to leave
87-117	Izmir, Turkey	2015 4 days from home	Dad, mom, smuggler And they are getting to Germany	a light drizzle making everything slick & damp	I think that this is a Dark war freedom
118-141	Izmir, Turkey	2015 11 days from home	Mahmoud, His sister, brother, mom, dad	Uncomfortable, fighting, cold	Safety
142-147	Havana Harbor	1939 17 days	Josef, sailor, Jewish passengers Josef got in trouble	frightening	Conflict be-Josef is getting in Sea fright
148-157	Mediterranean Sea	2015 11 days from home	Josef, Isabel, Mahmoud, Mahmoud is drowning	terror	because Mahmoud is about drown

Illustrate a few of the settings as a visual map of places the character went or where conflicts occurred. Use color to show the mood.

Page 104   Place Izmir Turkey   Mood renata (frightening)

Page 157   Place Mediterranean   Mood frightening

Figure 14.2.   Setting Mapper Example

an example of Supporting Caster and figure 14.2 for an example of Setting Master. Such role sheets help readers keep track of the names and places in *Refugee*.

For each meeting, students can choose the same or different role sheet. Every sheet is designed to encourage students to notice elements of plot and to document page numbers so that their questions are student generated but also text dependent, bringing student voices into conversation with the narrative. When questions are written in ways that can bring students to the text, students negotiate meaning, and when questions are written with aesthetic response in mind, students recognize the text as capable of stimulating emotions.

Finally, encouraging students to bring food to the book group meeting builds community. Together, they decided if they wanted food and who would bring what. The meal planning is a collaborative process and nurtures interdependence, ownership, comfort, and, well, fun.

Preparing for the Book Discussion: Reading

When preparing a week, use backward planning, which means working back from the book group discussion. Students need class time. Set aside a couple days for students to read in class almost the entire period. During this time, the teacher confers with students to check comprehension and talk through their notes.

It is important to make time in class for students to read. This is where and when the teacher can observe, support, and inform their reading habits. In every class, there are students who resist reading because of traumatic past experiences with reading logs or self-perceptions that they are not readers; this is an opportunity for the teacher to reframe reading alongside reluctant readers. By making time to read in class, every student will be prepared for the book group discussion and will feel a sense of belonging as a reader and member. Furthermore, teachers can monitor students' emotional responses to the sensitive content in *Refugee* and offer support as needed.

To conduct individual reading conferences on these days, simply have a notebook with a page for each student. Then walk around the room during reading time, kneel down beside a student, and say, "Tell me what's going on in your book right now." From there teachers can pose more questions: *Why do you think this is happening? How does this make you feel? What do you want to know more about?*

This is also the time to check students' progress on their roles to clarify the expectations and encourage them to find passages they want to discuss, process, interpret with their peers.

Preparing for Book Group Discussions: Research Day

In addition to reading days, plan for a day of research. Students reading *Refugee* want to know more about the Holocaust, the conflict in Cuba, and what was going on in Syria. Students also want to know about the "fiction" of historical fiction: what is fact and what is imagined by Alan Gratz. Individual reading conferences about *Refugee* will reveal anxiety about what will happen to the characters; this stems from past reading and learning experiences about the Holocaust.

One way to tell a reader is having anxiety about the story is when, during reading time, that reader turns ahead to upcoming chapters and scans for what's going to happen. Some students told me that they knew people died in the Holocaust, which meant people would die in *Refugee*, but they didn't know much about Isabel's Cuba or Mahmoud's Syria. So many questions emerge during the reading process, so a research day is a day of inquiry, a day to explore the gaps and fissures that are emerging for each reader.

Research begins with a few simple questions: What is a big concept the book explores? What do you want to know more about? The first time the class does this, prepare a mini-lesson on how to read news articles, and teach students how to learn more about and understand the impact of the organization publishing the article, the tone of the title, the biography of the writer, key terms, facts, statistics, and anecdotes. Encourage students to "read" the images for information. Students can take notes on a basic template and bring these to their book group discussions for easy reference.

For example, after reading the first seventy-five pages of *Refugee*, some students read an article from the UN Refugee Agency, "The world must not turn its back on the Syrian refugee crisis" (Grandi, 2017). One student wrote in her notes these words: explosive, conflict, ceasefires, and armed groups. She noted nearly 7,000 people were fleeing Syria every day. One image in the article shows UNHCR Chief Filippo Grandi walking past damaged buildings in eastern Aleppo and another shows a resident who fled Aleppo when the battle for the eastern parts began (Grandi, 2017).

Another student read an article, also from UNHCR, "Four Rohingya refugees die as boat capsizes off Bangladesh" (Tan, 2017). He describes the image in the article with these words: "crowded, people scared, children frightened, protest signs held by children." The detail he pulled from the article to discuss with his group was about how two thousand people waited in Gozon Dia for boats to take them to Bangladesh because they were afraid of military patrols that "sometimes take the girls away" (Tan, 2017, para.12).

This information enhanced the student's understanding of Isabel journey from Havana to Miami, and Mahmoud's journey from Izmir to Lesbos. Another student wanted to look up the story of Josef's MS. *St. Louis*, but he thought the research might spoil the story for him, so he opted for some research on Fidel Castro.

Book Discussion Day

On book discussion days, the energy of the class is palpable. Students drop off their books, move desks, and distribute their food and drinks. They all have their books, role sheets, and research notes, and they are ready to talk. With nearly thirty students, there can be six or more groups, so push the desks to the margins of the room to give as much intimacy and protection from sound as possible.

It is important for a teacher to hear every word without impacting student discussions, so groups can use digital recorders or recording extensions on their Chromebooks to record the discussions and post them on a class blog as evidence of learning. These recordings serve as artifacts for reflection, assessment, problem solving, and celebrating.

In the excerpt given next, students discuss the scene from *Refugee* when the dinghy taking Mahmoud and his family from Turkey to Greece capsizes and everyone, including Mahmoud's baby sister Hana, is trying to stay afloat. When another dinghy full of refugees comes by hours later, there is only enough room for baby Hana on the boat, and Mahmoud is able to convince a stranger to take her (book group discussion, Dec. 21, 2017):

Student 1: I want to hear your thought on page 195 and the word "wept." The denotation is "to express grief, sorrow, or any overpowering emotion by shedding tears." It says, "Mahmoud's mother fell to her knees on the rocky ground and wept, and Mahmoud's father held her close and let her cry." Why do you think she (Mahmoud's mom) was crying even though they survived the journey?

Student 2: In a mother's heart, when you let go of something, like your child, it's a big thing.

Student 3: Pages 192–96. It's the scene where they finally arrive on the Greece beach. Do you think this changes things for the better or worse? While they are in Greece, they still don't have Hana.

Student 1: I think this is worse because they still have to find citizenship, shelter over their heads, foods—all the basic necessities. Along with that, they lost a family member.

Student 4: I agree and disagree with Kyle. I am kind of in the middle. They should also feel lucky that they got to Europe safely even though they lost someone.

Student 1: I want to connect your question to an article. In this article the main person, Robert, back when he was a young child and going to his uncle's house, the rebels . . . met his uncle and thought he was a spy and killed him right on the spot. He mourned for his uncle like Mahmoud's mother was mourning for Hana. I would feel really sad if I lost a loved one.

Student 3: Your article is about a real event, and this book is not about a real person, but this stuff happened to people.

Their discussion went on for the entire forty minutes of class as they reread passages, pondered the nuance of words, and imagined how Josef, Isabel, and Mahmoud—kids their age—coped with the circumstance of their journey.

This next excerpt is from different *Refugee* book group, also seventh grade. Here, students discuss the ending of *Refugee* and react to how Alan Gratz (2017) resolved Josef's story (book group discussion, Nov. 17, 2018):

Student A: I think the ending was really clever because the stories came together. I liked how they ended with a cliffhanger for Josef how there's a choice whether. . . .

Student B: Cliffhanger? I liked how the author told what happened to Josef through Ruthie—she was telling her story to Mahmoud.

Student A: I also liked how Josef finally became a man—

Student C: By dying.

Student A: Yeah, by sacrificing himself.

Student C: One thing I didn't like about the ending was that Josef had to die so that Ruthie could survive. I wanted them all to survive.

Student D: I found it kind of cool that Ruthie was the grandmother who owned the house that Mahmoud and his family would stay in and that she was a toy designer. Remember when she was little she always had that stuffed bunny? That makes sense.

Listening to the recording of this discussion, one can note the contrast of the harsh reality in the death of Josef, which one boy could express in this discussion, and the innocent symbolism in Ruthie's bunny, which seems like Alan Gratz's (2017) way of softening the unimaginable choice Josef's mother made in saving Ruthie that fateful day.

In the end of *Refugee*, Ruthie comforts Mahmoud by explaining the sacrifices family makes for loved ones: "They died so I could live. Do you understand? They died so all these people could live. All the grandchildren and nieces and nephews they never got to meet. But you'll get to meet them," she told Mahmoud (Gratz, 2017, p. 316). And the book group members did the same for one another in the way they listened to one another, the way they looked for answers to one another's questions, the way they tried to make sense of the conflicts and emotions of the characters.

CAUTIONS AND ADVICE

Some teachers are just not comfortable reading human rights literature with students because of the violence and its political nature. One of the goals of any literature class is to teach students to make their way through the stories of humanity in meaningful ways. To avoid literary violence is to miss out on the ideas, politics, and social forces that have moved civilization.

Still, reading about a character's death is emotional. In Matt de la Peña's (2018) article "Why We Shouldn't Shield Children From Darkness," he suggests, "Maybe instead of anxiously trying to protect our children from every little hurt and heartache, our job is simply to support them through such experiences. To talk to them. To hold them" (para. 12). While de la Peña's (2018) article was specifically about elementary-aged children, teen readers also certainly need opportunities to talk about the sense of loss, the sadness, the sympathy.

CONCLUSION

Literature can teach us *about* refugee experiences. *Refugee* troubles any easy notion of there being a single refugee story by including three and making visible how every story has implications beyond the journey, past the arrival, and into generations. The reading process, however, is enriched when teachers model their classrooms after a narrative like *Refugee* by welcoming student voices in the reading, analysis, research, and discussions. A cooperative reading approach takes planning:

- Make time for reading in class so that teachers can confer during the reading experience.
- Create role sheets to help students focus on text structure and choose what passages to they'd like to discuss.
- Teach research skills to explore questions and extend understanding.
- Support students as they draw from their reading experiences to share and extend understanding with a community of readers.

Teachers can help young readers uncover dimensions of humanity and trouble how the word tries to represent the world, and they can also support readers as they grapple with literary loss and grief. This does, however, take careful planning and trust in the students to find both personal and social meaning in what they read.

BOX 14.1   CONNECTED RESOURCES

Abawi, A. (2018). *A land of permanent goodbyes*. New York, NY: Philomel Books.

Abawi focuses on one boy's refugee journey from Syria to Greece. The narrative style is similar to *The Book Thief* in that the refugee journey is narrated by Destiny.

Anderson, N. (2017). *City of saints and thieves*. New York, NY: G.P. Putnam's Sons Books for Young Readers.

Anderson offers readers a story of life as a Kenyan refugee in the Congo. This main character, Tina, survives on the streets alone, working for a local gang and trying to uncover the truth of her mother's death.

Sepetys, R. (2016). *Salt to the sea*. New York, NY: Philomel Books.

Like *Refugee*, *Salt to the Sea* includes multiple narrators: four young people with their own stories bound together by their desperation to reach a ship that will take them to safety; however, this story is also based on a true, heartbreaking story from World War II of a German ship that sunk in port with over 9,000 refugees.

Diaz, A. (2017). *The only road*. New York, NY: Simon & Schuster.

Inspired by true events, *The Only Road* is one story of a boy who leaves his home in Guatemala to escape the local gang pressuring kids to work for them. The book emerged out of the sudden influx of Central and South American refugees coming to the United States.

Williams, M. (2011). *Now is the time for running*. New York, NY: Little, Brown Books for Young Readers.

When the soldiers came to his Zimbabwe village, one boy took his brother and ran from the civil war to a refugee camp in South Africa where soccer becomes a safe haven.

REFERENCES

de la Peña's, M. (2018, January 8). Why we shouldn't shield children from darkness. *Time.* Retrieved from http://time.com/5093669/why-we-shouldnt-shield-children-from-darkness/?xid=homepage

Freire, P., & Macedo, D. (1987). *Literacy: Reading the word and the world.* South Hadley, MA: Bergin & Garvey.

Grandi, F. (2017, October 16). The world must not turn its back on the Syrian refugee crisis. *UNHCR: The UN Refugee Agency.* Retrieved from http://www.unhcr.org/en-us/news/latest/2017/10/59e61a584/world-must-turn-its-syrian-refugee-crisis.html

Gratz, A. (2017). *Refugee.* New York, NY: Scholastic Press.

Tan, V. (2017, October 31). Four Rohingya refugees die as boat capsizes off Bangladesh. *UNHCR: The UN Refugee Agency.* Retrieved from http://www.unhcr.org/en-us/news/latest/2017/10/59f87e754/four-rohingya-refugees-die-boat-capsizes-bangladesh.html

About the Editors

Michelle M. Falter is an assistant professor of English education in the Department of Teacher Education and Learning Sciences within the College of Education at North Carolina State University, in Raleigh, North Carolina. Previously, Michelle worked as a middle and high school English teacher for ten years in Wisconsin, abroad in Germany, and the Dominican Republic, and also as a high school instructional coach in Georgia before becoming a teacher educator. She is also a National Writing Project teaching consultant and advocate. Michelle has won several awards for teaching and scholarship, including the Nilsen-Donelson Award for the Best Article of the Year in 2016 in *ALAN Review*, which recognizes excellence in scholarship in the field of young article literature. She has coedited a book titled *Teaching Outside the Box but Inside the Standards: Making Room for Dialogue* with Teachers College Press, along with co/authoring numerous articles. She currently serves on the Commission for the Study and Teaching of Adolescent Literature within the Conference on English Education (CEE) and the Committee against Racism and Bias in the Teaching of English within NCTE. Michelle's scholarship focuses on dialogic, critical, and feminist pedagogies, English teacher education, adolescent literature, and emotion in the teaching of literature and writing in secondary classrooms.

Steven T. Bickmore is associate professor of English education in the Department of Teaching and Learning in the College of Education at the University of Nevada, Las Vegas (UNLV). He taught high school English in the Jordan School District in the Salt Lake City area from 1980 to 2008. In addition to teaching English courses, including Advanced Placement courses, he taught Latin and humanities. His many teacher awards and recognitions included an NEH/Reader's Digest Teacher Scholar Award (a full-year paid research sabbatical) for the 1989–1990 school year, and he was a winner of the prestigious Milken Educator Award in 1999. He is a cofounder and coeditor of *Study and Scrutiny: Research in Young Adult Literature*. Also, he was a coeditor of *The ALAN Review* from 2009 to 2014. Bickmore began his university teaching at Louisiana State University in 2008 before moving to UNLV in 2015. He has authored or coauthored over thirty academic papers and book chapters and published in a variety of journals. He maintains an academic blog Dr. Bickmore's YA Wednesday that discusses the teaching and research of young adult literature.

About the Contributors

Steven T. Bickmore is associate professor of English education at the University of Nevada, Las Vegas (UNLV). He taught high school English in the Jordan School District in the Salt Lake City from 1980 to 2008. In addition to teaching English courses, including advanced placement courses, he taught Latin and humanities. His many teacher awards and recognitions included an NEH/Reader's Digest Teacher Scholar Award (a full-year paid research sabbatical) for the 1989–1990 school year, and he was a winner of the prestigious Milken Educator Award in 1999. He is a cofounder and coeditor of *Study and Scrutiny: Research in Young Adult Literature*. He was also a coeditor of *ALAN Review* from 2009 to 2014. He maintains an academic blog Dr. Bickmore's YA Wednesday that discuss the teaching and research of young adult literature.

Ashley S. Boyd is an assistant professor of English education at Washington State University where she teaches courses on critical theory, English methods, and young adult literature. Her research interests include critical literacies, social justice pedagogies, and tribal curriculum in secondary schools, and she recently published *Social Justice Literacies in the English Classroom: Teaching Practice in Action* with Teachers College Press.

James Joshua Coleman is a doctoral candidate in the Reading/Writing/Literacy program at the University of Pennsylvania's Graduate School of Education. Specializing in LGBT and queer-themed young adult literature, he researches intersectional issues of representation in graphic and tradition print texts. Some of his academic areas of interest include young adult literature, queer theory and studies, affect studies, and critical literacy.

Tiye Naeemah Cort is a PhD student in curriculum and instruction at the University of Texas at Austin. She has taught in independent schools in Boston, Massachusetts, Dublin, New Hampshire, and Austin, Texas. Her research interests include literacy, social media, and reading and writing identity in black women. She runs a personal blog *The Black Educator* at www. theblackeducator.com, where she writes about education and other lifestyle topics. She is also the founder of *Feminessay*, and online writing community for Black women writers.

Kellie Crawford is an elementary teacher in Spokane, Washington. She currently teaches both first and second grades. She is pursuing her master of education at Eastern Washington University. Her research focuses on the effect of public schools' partnerships with informal science institutions on student achievement and student attitudes toward science instruction.

Jennifer S. Dail is a professor of English education in the Department of English at Kennesaw State University in Kennesaw, Georgia. She also directs the Kennesaw Mountain Writing Project (KMWP), a National Writing Project site serving teachers Pre-K through college in all content areas. Dail served as coeditor of *SIGNAL Journal*, from 2008 to 2013. She serves on the board for the Georgia Council of Teachers of English as the interim conference director and college liaison. Dail has published multiple articles on young adult literature and technology in the *ALAN Review* and has several book chapters focusing on this work as well.

Janine Julianna Darragh is an assistant professor of literacy and English as a Second Language at the University of Idaho where she instructs courses in young adult literature, English and ESL methods, and content literacy. Her research interests are sociocultural and social justice issues in teaching and learning, and her current scholarship is focused on supporting teachers of refugees and teachers in rural Nicaraguan schools.

Sarah J. Donovan is a junior high English language arts (ELA) teacher and adjunct professor in teacher education at DePaul University. She is the author of *Genocide Literature in Middle and Secondary Classrooms* and a young adult novel *Alone Together*. She writes a weekly blog, Ethical ELA, where she explores the ethics of teaching English and shares young adult book reviews.

Amye Ellsworth earned her BA in English from Eastern Washington University. She then earned her master of arts in teaching from Eastern Washington University in 2017, focusing her studies on elementary education. Her research project for the master's program focused on the use of hip-hop in the elementary school classroom. Currently, she teaches second grade in Cheney, Washington.

Cathlin Goulding is a Mellon postdoctoral research fellow at the 9/11 Memorial & Museum and a visiting scholar at New York University. Currently, she studies how site-specific cultural institutions translate historical violence for the public. She previously worked as a high school English teacher and has an EdD in curriculum and teaching from Teachers College, Columbia University.

Stephanie P. Jones is an assistant professor of education at Grinnell College, a private liberal arts college in the Midwest. She currently teaches methods courses for prospective English teachers along with special topics courses such as reading and writing youth cultures, risky texts, and critical literacy for diverse learners. Her research interests are situated in black girls' literacy practices within urban contemporary young adult literature and also the ways in which racial trauma is embedded in classroom spaces and curriculums.

Crystal Chen Lee is an assistant professor of ELA and literacy at North Carolina State University. Her research lies at the nexus of literacy, historically underserved youth, and community organizations. A former high school English teacher, she received her EdD in curriculum and teaching from Teachers College, Columbia University.

Mark A. Lewis is an associate professor of literacy education at Loyola University Maryland, where he teaches courses in children's and young adult literature, content area literacy, and English methods. His research examines literary competence and conceptions of youth in secondary ELA teaching and learning, as well as critically analyzes representations of youth and adolescence in young adult literature.

Jackie Mercer has been a high school English teacher in rural northeast Ohio for eight years. Ms. Mercer has participated in several workshops across the country that are focused on civil rights and social justice. Ms. Mercer is also a member of NCTE and has presented at the national conference. Social justice is one of her primary passions.

Leilya Pitre is a former ELA / English secondary school teacher. Currently, she is an assistant professor of English education at Southeastern Louisiana University where she teaches content methods courses for English education majors, American literature, and young adult literature. Her research interests include teacher preparation, early field experiences, and teaching of young adult and multicultural literature.

Gretchen Rumohr-Voskuil is a department chair, associate professor of English, and writing program administrator at Aquinas College in Grand Rapids, Michigan, where she teaches writing and English methods courses.

René Saldaña, Jr. is an associate professor of language, diversity, and literacy studies at Texas Tech University. Saldaña is the author of several novels and short story collections for tweens and teen readers. His titles include *The Jumping Tree*, *Finding Our Way: Stories*, *The Whole Sky Full of Stars*, *A Good Long Way*, and the bilingual *Mickey Rangel* detective series.

Lindsay Schneider earned her BA in English and political science as well as her MEd in secondary English education from Wake Forest University. She currently teaches AP literature and composition and English IV at West Forsyth High School in Winston-Salem, North Carolina, and is an active member of NCTE and ALAN.

Shelly Shaffer is an assistant professor of literacy in the department of education at Eastern Washington University, Cheney, Washington, where she teaches preservice elementary and secondary teachers and graduate students in education. Dr. Shaffer taught middle school and high school English for thirteen years in Arizona until she earned her PhD in English education from Arizona State University in 2015. Her current research interests are young adult literature, reading motivation, flipped classrooms, mentoring, and multimedia integration in teacher education programs.

Deborah Vriend Van Duinen is a former high school English teacher and now an associate professor of English education at Hope College in Holland, Michigan. In addition to working with secondary preservice teachers, Deborah is also the program director of the Big Read Lakeshore.

Shelbie Witte is the Kim and Chuck Watson Endowed Chair in Education and associate professor of adolescent literacy and English education at Oklahoma State University, where she directs the Oklahoma State University Writing Project and leads the Initiative for 21st Century Literacies Research. Her research focuses on the intersection of twenty-first-century literacies and pedagogy, particularly at the middle level. She is coeditor, along with Sara Kajder, of NCTE's *Voices from the Middle*.

Index

26, 27, 29, 30; for *Mockingbird*, 80–81; for *Pedro and Me*, 24, 25–33, *26, 27, 29, 30*; on rites of passage, 15–16; for short stories, 15–16; for *The Things They Carried*, 115–17; for *THUG*, *51*, 51–53, 54
primitivism, 34n1
"the Prince" (fictional character), 13–14
Probst, Robert E., 68, 115
PTSD. *See* post-traumatic stress disorder
Purple Heart, 127

queer, 34n3
questions: as authentic, 119, *120*; for *Drowned City*, 104–5; for *The Things They Carried*, 119, *120*
quilt, 157
"Quinn Collins" (fictional character), 38–45, *43*

"Rachel Landau" (fictional character), 163
racialized trauma, 40
racism. *See All American Boys*; *Getting Away with Murder*
Racism Is Real, 42
RAFT. *See* Role, Audience, Format, Topic
Rampage (Newman, Fox, Harding, Mehta, and Roth), 93
"Rashad Butler" (fictional character), 38–45, *43*
reading: as close, 64–70, *69*; as cooperative, 165–75, *167, 168, 169*; of visual images, 106–7. *See also* critical reading; During Reading strategies; postreading; prereading; specific literature
Reagan, Ronald, 23
reaggregation, 14
The Real World: San Francisco, 24–33, *26, 27, 29, 30*
recursive mapping, 8–9
Red Cross, 141–43
Reddit, 85
reflection, 130–32
Refugee (Gratz): book groups, 163–75,

167, 168, 169; cautions and advice for, 174; character death in, 163–75, *167, 168, 169*; comfort and, 163–75, *167, 168, 169*; cooperative reading approach to, 165–75, *167, 168, 169*; discomfort and, 163–75, *167, 168, 169*; discussions for, 166–73, *167, 168, 169*; overview of, 163–75, *167, 168, 169*; preparing for, 170–71; During Reading strategies for, 170; research for, 170–71; resources connected to, 175; small groups for, 166–70, *167, 168, 169*
relationship/reaction discussions, 55
religion, *Elsewhere* influencing, 9–10
research: for *Mockingbird*, 80–81, 83–84; for *Refugee*, 170–71
resources: *All American Boys* connected to, 45; *Drowned City* connected to, 109; *Elsewhere* connected to, 11; *Getting Away with Murder* connected to, 72; *A Long Way Gone* connected to, 146; *Maus* connected to, 161; *Mockingbird* connected to, 86; *Night* connected to, 161; *Pedro and Me* connected to, 33; *Refugee* connected to, 175; *A Separate Peace* connected to, 134; short stories connected to, 21; *The Things They Carried* connected to, 122; *This Is Where It Ends* connected to, 99; *THUG* connected to, 61
Reynolds, Jason, 37–45, *43*
Rice, David, 14–21
Rice, Tamir, 69
rites of passage, 15–16
"Robert" (fictional character), 172
Role, Audience, Format, Topic (RAFT), 97
role-playing, 15–20
Romano, Tom, 119, 121
"Romeo" (fictional character), 13–14, 37
Romeo and Juliet (Shakespeare), 13–14
Rosenblatt, L. M., 95, 96
Roth, W., 93

War Journal writing activity, 130–32
"We do" section, 30–31
White, Brian, 119
whiteness, 70–72
whole-class discussion, 55–56, *56*
"Why We Shouldn't Shield Children From Darkness" (Peña), 174
Wiesel, Elie, 149–61, *157, 158, 160*
Williams, Patricia, 39–40
Winick, Judd, 23–33, *26, 27, 29, 30*
Winn, Maisha, 41–42
witness, Starr Carter as, 50
witnessing, 149–61, *157, 158, 160*
Witte, Shelbie, 101–9
word connotator, 166, *167*
World War II (WWII). *See Maus; Night; A Separate Peace*
Wright, Simeon, 68–69
writing: as collaborative, 153–54; for critical literacy, 96–97; to heal, 130–32; *Letter from the War* activity

of, 130–32; for *Night*, 153–54; to reflect, 130–32; for *A Separate Peace*, 130–32; for *This Is Where It Ends*, 96–97; *War Journal* activity of, 130–32; as witnessing, 153–54
writing prompts: as autobiographical, 116; for *The Things They Carried*, 116; for *THUG*, *51*, 52–53
WWII. *See Maus; Night; A Separate Peace*

YAL. *See specific literature*
"You Do" section, 31
young adult literature (YAL). *See specific literature*
Youngstown, Ohio, 71–72
YouTube, 42

Zamora, Pedro, 25–33, *26, 27, 29, 30*
Zevin, Gabrielle, 3–11, *7–8*
Zimmerman, George, 37–38